The Karting Manual

Second Edition

For Charlotte, Jude and Etienne

Acknowledgements

My sincere gratitude to Ian Berry, whose considerable knowledge and advice laid the foundation for the first edition of this book; Chris Walker for promptly supplying a range of images that effortlessly complement the contributions of first edition photographers Enver Meyer, Darren Bourne and Greg Richardson; Paul Edwards, for revisiting and enhancing his previous illustrative work; Tom Gaymor, Greg Symes and Tom Onslow-Cole at the MSA Academy for their invaluable insight, echoed in a number of key chapters; Steve Cooper at the McLaren Press Office for his kind assistance and Jenson Button for again graciously agreeing to the foreword. Last but by no means least, my thanks to Mark Hughes and Steve Rendle at Haynes for their understanding and support throughout this second edition.

First published in March 2007
Second edition published in June 2011
Reprinted August 2012 and June 2013

British Library Cataloguing in Publication Data:
A catalogue record for this book is available from the British Library

ISBN 978 0 85733 086 4

Library of Congress catalog card no. 2010943422

Published by Haynes Publishing, Sparkford, Yeovil, Somerset BA22 7JJ, UK
Tel: 01963 442030 Fax: 01963 440001
Int. tel: +44 1963 442030 Int. fax: +44 1963 440001
E-mail: sales@haynes.co.uk
Website: www.haynes.co.uk

Haynes North America Inc.
861 Lawrence Drive, Newbury Park,
California 91320, USA

Printed in the USA by Odcombe Press LP
1299 Bridgestone Parkway, La Vergne, TN 37086

All photographs supplied by Enver Meyer Photography, unless otherwise credited.
Cover photograph by Chris Walker.

The Karting Manual

Second Edition

The complete beginner's guide to competitive kart racing

João Diniz Sanches

FOREWORD BY JENSON BUTTON

Foreword
BY JENSON BUTTON

I feel very privileged to be asked to write this Foreword because I have great memories of my time racing karts. While I enjoyed a lot of success over a period of 10 years, I also had a great deal of fun. I made a lot of friends among the drivers, some of whom I'm still racing in Formula One today.

My father gave me a kart for Christmas in 1987 and I started racing it the following year, at the age of eight. Being so young, I absorbed information like a sponge and that knowledge has stood me in good stead ever since.

Karting taught me all the basics of being a racing driver, but two important lessons in particular: to be dedicated and to deal with setbacks. I won a lot of races and championships, culminating with my victory in European Super A in 1997, but I still had

bad days and it was important to deal with those disappointments and to move on.

I still try to get on a kart whenever I can, but I'm on the road so much in F1 – either travelling or testing – that I rarely get the chance. For now, I'll leave the karting to you, the readers of this excellent karting manual by João Diniz Sanches. He provides a comprehensive insight into the sport, which is relevant to all levels of ability and budget.

I believe that karting is the best way to get involved in motorsport. Enjoy yourselves and I hope you have as much fun as I did.

Jenson

ABOVE
Jenson pilots his Tecno kart at Salbris, France in 1997, on his way to becoming the youngest ever winner of the European Super A Championship. *(sutton-images.com)*

BELOW The skills learnt in karting are invaluable, and can be adapted and applied at the pinnacle of motorsport – Jenson battles with Fernando Alonso during the 2010 Malaysian Grand Prix. *(LAT)*

Introduction

Karting is one of the best forms of motorsport. This isn't because it's tremendous fun and relatively cheap, or the fact it typically offers some of the most exciting racing around. Or even that it's universally embracing, meaning that whether you're young or old, male or female, disabled or otherwise, there'll be a kart you can race. It's because of all of those things and more.

The first time you drive a racing kart it will be a revelation. It doesn't matter how many cars you may have driven or ridden in, nothing will have matched the thrill of buzzing along at 60mph or more, some five centimetres off the ground. No other form of four-wheeled motorsport can either, because no other vehicle can boast of having the directional responses of a fly and spine-tingling acceleration, combined with keeping you as close and open to the elements. It's a tremendous mix.

It isn't just about thrills, though. These days, karting provides the backbone of all forms of motorsport, a place where future rally, touring car or Formula One champions learn the fundamentals of their trade and acquire the experience that will serve them for the rest of their racing career.

That may be indisputable, but it is imperative to think of karting as more than just a stepping stone to other motorised formulae. It is an excellent and worthy sport in its own right, with huge (and growing) support, increasing exposure (it's now featured regularly on digital television sports channels), and provides some of the best action-

packed, furiously competitive, wheel-to-wheel racing on the planet.

There's a purity to this sport, clearly influenced by the relative simplicity of a kart's construction, that is intoxicating. Of the many drivers who come to karting with the intention of progressing on to other forms of motorsport, many never make it any further. This is not because they don't have the talent, but because they enjoy karting too much to go on to something else that may ultimately fail to deliver the same kick, so frequently. Karting is relentlessly exhilarating, and you'll have to climb a very, very long way up the motorsport ladder before you obtain as intense an emotion from your machinery. And the beauty, of course, is that you don't have to.

This book has been put together with the aim of helping those new to competitive karting by covering all the fundamental elements of the sport. Where appropriate, the content takes a deliberately straightforward approach to some of karting's more technical aspects, so as to maximise its utility to drivers displaying even the most basic level of mechanical knowledge. With that in mind, as they increase their karting experience readers are encouraged to consult some of the publications that deal with specific technical aspects such as set-up, in far more detail than space allows here – many of the following chapters would fill a book on their own. But there's

many racing miles and far too much fun to be had before then.

That last point is crucial. Whatever you do, enjoy yourself – karting is one of the most exciting and rewarding activities you can do on four wheels. And best of all, you can trust it to deliver this time and time again, regardless of the level at which you compete.

RIGHT A vintage kart bearing relevance to today's machinery, not least in its use of a tubular chassis *(Author)*

INDOOR VS OUTDOOR

BELOW An example of a high-performance 'arrive and drive' two-stroke kart; a far cry from the corporate karts of indoor circuits *(Author)*

With most indoor kart circuits catering for an increasing number of events these days – anything from birthday parties to 'stag dos' to corporate team-building exercises – it is generally the case that most people's first karting experience will come from a visit to such a track.

Some, their curiosity sated, may not feel the need to ever get into a kart again. Everyone else, however, is likely to be counting the days until they next find themselves behind the wheel.

A number of these individuals may actually bypass indoor karting immediately, focusing instead on locating their nearest outdoor circuit (there are considerably fewer of these than their indoor equivalent, but then you do know what they say about quantity and quality). Others may take a little more convincing, and are likely to choose to remain racing protected from the elements for a considerably longer period of time and, indeed, may never make the transition.

And that would a shame, because as enjoyable as indoor karting can be, it really just represents a glimpse of what this sport is able to offer when freed from the restraints of a warehouse or hangar. The differences can be colossal, in fact, and for those still wondering what all the fuss is about, some of these have been highlighted below.

Speed

The most obvious difference, perhaps. While indoor kart circuits will often advertise machinery capable of 40mph, the reality at most tracks is more likely to hover below 30mph. Not that this doesn't feel fast when you're travelling a few centimetres off the ground, of course.

But consider the fact that once outdoors even hire karts can get you past 50mph, while race karts will often return speeds of between 60–80mph (superkarts, for those sufficiently brave, will actually top 150mph), depending on the category being raced.

As you'd expect, the way in which you reach the top speed on an 'outdoor' kart is also different, with most two-stroke-engined karts offering brutal levels of acceleration.

Grip level

Aside from often running on smooth concrete (or worse), indoor karts are normally fitted with the hardest rubber-compound tyres available in order to guarantee the longest lifespan before a new set of boots is needed, thereby keeping running costs under control. And the problem with hard tyres, as you'll see in Chapter 9, is that they offer little grip. Combined with a slippery surface, it's certainly a recipe for a lot of sideways fun, though not exactly what you'd call racing.

Obviously, good indoor circuits exist, just as there are poor outdoor equivalents. Generally, however, a dedicated surface, better tyres and the use of more advanced chassis means that even outdoor 'arrive and drive' (hire) karting will seem a world away from any indoor experience you may have had. There tends to be no comparison in the level of grip available, with outdoor karting immediately feeling a lot more akin to real racing.

Chassis characteristics

While it's not akin to comparing a Ferrari to, say, a tractor, the difference between a race kart chassis and an indoor kart frame is enormous. The two may look similar to a beginner but where an indoor kart has been built to be used and abused by clients and is little more than a glorified bumper car (and is therefore by definition an unwieldy beast designed for a life of relentless corporate hire), a race kart chassis is the result of a remarkable level of development aimed at extracting the maximum performance from the kart's other components. Race chassis are far more agile and offer far more sophisticated levels of handling, as well as more noticeable differences between one manufacturer's creation and another.

Cost

It shouldn't come as a surprise to learn that outdoor hire karting costs more than its indoor cousin (owner karting is another world of expenditure entirely, and is looked at in Chapter 2). However, it's worth mentioning that the additional sum usually paid for the privilege is disproportionate to the additional level of enjoyment you will experience. In other words, outdoor karting provides more fun for your money.

Level of competition

No one is disputing that indoor karting can't offer a

LEFT Cost-controlling initiatives are becoming increasingly common, and include attractive all-in-one packages for those wishing to get into the ownership of competitive machinery without needing absurd budgets. *(Author)*

racing experience. At the right track and in the right company, it absolutely can – just witness the level of competition at events such as the Johnny Herbert Karting Challenge yearly charity race, for instance, which pits stars of the world of motorsport against everyday karters and is held at an indoor circuit.

It's just that if you're serious about racing karts, or even if you're just looking to emulate the inimitable thrill of motorsport, you'll soon realise how limited the indoor experience is. All major competitions – and competitors – can be found on outdoor tracks. That's where the real challenge lies, and the only place you'll discover what kart racing is really about.

BELOW A world championship-winning chassis package represents the pinnacle of karting, and delivers the kind of performance only the highest categories of single-seater motorsport are able to match. *(Author)*

(Photo: Chris Walker)

1

The karting scene

Introduction

The first kart was imagined and manufactured by Art Ingels and Lou Borelli in the USA, way back in August 1956. Ingels, a race car builder, used to drive the simple creation (which used a surplus two-stroke engine mounted on the most basic tubular chassis rolling along on semi-pneumatic tyres) around his local car parks.

It wasn't long before others began to show great interest in this fun little invention and by 1957, the first kart manufacturing companies started appearing in North America.

Within a year, the craze had spread to the UK, mainly through American servicemen stationed here. Subsequent demonstrations at some of the nation's racing circuits further boosted karting's popularity and the sport took off through the 1960s, '70s and '80s, helped along by the emergence of more sophisticated chassis design, better braking systems, wider tyres and general safety improvements.

The 1980s saw a more significant arrival still, in the form of indoor circuits hosting low-powered yet fun karts that members of the public could easily experience. Until then, only those individuals holding a racing licence were allowed behind the wheel of a kart, which they could then race at a limited number of outdoor tracks. This, along with a further key evolution in the form of a cadet class for children aged eight years onwards, contributed significantly to karting's rapidly rising popularity.

ABOVE The modern premier karting classes may benefit from decades of technological evolution, but they still share the fundamental concepts of the very first karts. *(Chris Walker)*

By the mid-1990s it had become the UK's fastest-growing sport and it didn't take long for the rest of Europe – and subsequently neighbouring continents – to catch up. These days you'll find kart circuits in or near just about any major city in the world.

Along with a global explosion in indoor centres, some recognised the potential of enabling non-licence holders access to the type of more powerful and better handling machinery being raced on the outdoor tracks as the next logical step.

The interest in karting hasn't shown any signs of slowing down since.

Karting associations

Different organisations look after the interests of karting and regulate the sport in different parts of the world. Internationally, the main sanctioning body is the CIK-FIA (Commission Internationale de Karting – Fédération Internationale de l'Automobile) and it oversees a number of national events in a variety of countries, as well as leading multinational competitions such as the Karting World Championship.

In the UK, as with other forms of motorsport, karting falls under the control of the MSA, the Motor Sports Association, which establishes a strict set of regulations to which both event organisers and competitors must adhere when engaged in officially recognised competitions. (In addition to the MSA, there are a number of national organisations dedicated to karting. Information and contact details for the major examples of these can be found in Appendix 2.)

Over in North America, the largest body regulating kart racing is the World Karting Association (WKA). Although not as big, the International Kart Federation (IKF) was actually the first kart racing organisation in the US and has published its rules for competition since 1957 – the year that kart manufacturing began. With the CIK-FIA not as involved in North America, both the WKA and IKF regulate some of the higher profile kart racing meetings, although many other associations are involved at all levels of North American events.

In other countries, a national organisation will at times oversee the sport on behalf of the CIK-FIA, but other associations can and do exist, of course. Your local circuit should be able to provide the necessary information or you can obtain this by doing a quick search online. (You'll also find a number of national karting associations listed in Appendix 2.)

Types of event

Indoor

The growth of indoor kart centres around the world has been remarkable and they now represent a standard corporate entertainment option. Most offer a low-speed, slippery yet fun experience, but there are decent tracks with a dedicated surface delivering something of a glimpse into the fundamentals of karting. It is a long, long way from getting behind the wheel of a

ABOVE Indoor karting had a huge effect on boosting the popularity of karting. *(Enver Meyer)*

BELOW Most outdoor circuits provide fun corporate versions of racing karts. *(Enver Meyer)*

race-spec kart, but it is certainly enjoyable enough
to spur many people to progress on to the outdoor
tracks and therefore come closer to finding out the
true potential of a kart.

Outdoor

Outdoor circuits are where 'real' karting began and
has remained, but it had previously been only
frequented by those with racing licences. This
created a substantial barrier for anyone intrigued by
the sport, but not necessarily prepared to commit at
that level yet. It is only in the last decade or so that
ordinary members of the public have been given the
chance to try out more powerful karts on outdoor
circuits without the need for a licence, due to the
forward-thinking approach of one or two companies.
It is a concept that has since seen most major UK
kart tracks following suit, and 'arrive-and-drive'
outdoor events are now numerous (see below).

Outdoor tracks are further divided into short and
long circuits. Short circuits are specifically designed
karting venues hosting direct drive (no gears) and
gearbox kart meetings, and typically measure
between 800m to 1200m in length. Long circuit
karting is almost exclusive based around the faster
gearbox classes and takes place at some of the
major UK circuits used by other categories of
motorsport.

A similar approach is employed in karting nations
across the world, with only the typical length of
short circuits as the most significant difference.

Sprint

Sprint events are normally contested by individual
competitors over a series of short heats (often just
six to eight laps), followed by a slightly longer final.
Depending on the number of drivers, there may be
two (or more) finals, split into A and B, with some
of the top finishing drivers of the B final joining the
back of the A event. Sprint races tend to be the
preferred format for two-stroke-powered karts
because of the fact it suits the typically short-
running characteristic of their engines.

Endurance

These are longer races, ranging from one to 24
hours and usually adhering to a team-based format
(with a designated minimum number of drivers per
team dependent on the event). Normally the domain
of four-stroke engine-powered karts due to their
longer-running ability, endurance events offer a
considerable physical and mental challenge and
have gained popularity in recent years.

In the US, endurance events can be
considerably different from their European
counterpart. 'Enduro' meetings are typically run
without pit stops in races lasting 30 or 45 minutes
but also take place on full-size circuits and can
employ radically different looking machinery
('Laydown Enduro' karts feature low drag bodywork
and require the driver to lie almost flat on their back).

Speedway

Mainly very popular in North America, speedway
kart races occur on oval tracks between ⅛ mile and
¼ mile long, surfaced in either asphalt or clay. As
with NASCAR vehicles, Speedway karts are
specifically designed and set up to handle the
circuit's left-only turns. Although of limited relevance
in terms of the focus of this book, it is nevertheless
another form of karting and the action can be
thrilling. (It can also be found outside of the USA –
Stoxkart racing in the UK, for instance, has a
relatively small but devoted following.)

ABOVE Senior Rotax Max is a very popular series for experienced drivers. *(Enver Meyer)*

BELOW New, higher performance four-stroke engines exist, but Honda-powered prokarts remain popular for endurance events. *(Greg Richardson)*

Arrive and drive

These events were one of the breakthroughs at the end of the last century, enabling non-licence holders the chance to control powerful race karts on outdoor circuits – a far cry from what they were used to at their local indoor track. They are almost always based around a single-make series, the idea being this ensures there is as little performance discrepancy between drivers as a result of placing them all behind the wheel of identical machinery. Most locations will run both sprint and endurance formats, with drivers effectively hiring a race seat for a day: they pay their money, turn up at the circuit, and the kart is already prepped, set up and ready to go. It's a cost-effective way of sampling performance karting before taking the plunge. Or, often, the ideal solution for someone without the time, funds or inclination to get involved with the intricacies of owning their own kart, but who nevertheless relishes an opportunity to race rewarding machinery (the standard of driving in some series can be exceptional).

Officially licensed events

Run by officially recognised clubs, these are meetings that adhere to the competition guidelines set up by the governing body. In the UK, for instance, these encompass all of the national and regional MSA-approved events and require a licence from competitors taking part (this is detailed in the next chapter). Meetings are bound by strict guidelines and will run with an MSA representative, ensuring aspects relating to procedure, legality, safety and driving standards are observed. MSA events guarantee the presence of marshals and a full paramedic team. In many series, it's not unusual to have drivers separated in terms of their experience via 'clubman' and 'expert' designations, for instance, yet racing on the track at the same time.

Non-licensed events

Primarily the realm of the arrive-and-drive races that prove particularly attractive to those who may be looking to get involved with karting on a more leisurely level. Overall standards can lapse at some clubs and you're unlikely to be able to rely on medical cover as with an MSA event, but many are run in a highly professional manner and offer excellent competitive racing.

Types of kart

A number of types of karts exist – from electric to jet power and raced on anything from dirt to snow – but within the context of this book, outdoor karts run in competitions around the world are broadly divided into two types: two-stroke and four-stroke. The engines (along with other components such as carburettor, chassis, and tyres) then determine the level of performance you can expect. Whichever category of kart you go for, you'll have to factor in engine rebuilds at regular intervals. As with all race engines, the components in kart engines endure great stresses and general wear and tear under racing or testing conditions and as such require a little tender love and care in order to maintain/regain their optimal performance. The type of engine will determine the frequency of the rebuilds, with the higher performing units usually suffering from the shortest running time.

Two-stroke karts

By far the most popular type of kart run competitively worldwide, two-stroke-engined machines are generally noisier and have a limited running time compared with their four-stroke cousins (hence the reason why sprint races are predominant in these classes) and have traditionally required larger budgets, not least as a result of the more frequent engine rebuilds or replacements necessary. Recent years have see an number of incentives and new classes aimed at introducing elements that control some of the costs (such as the Touch-and-Go (TAG) 125cc engines equipped with an electric start button which are now used extensively throughout the leading classes, run for longer between rebuilds and can also be 'sealed' units to prevent competitors getting into the exorbitant world of tuning options, for example). When not featuring a clutch (direct-drive), most two-stroke karts have traditionally required a push start although this is increasingly less common as the use of dry centrifugal clutches is rapidly becoming the norm in modern direct-drive kart engines.

Four-stroke karts

Renowned for their ease of maintenance, reliability and cost-friendly nature due to the impressively durable operation of their engines, the popularity of sprint four-stroke events has nevertheless dwindled. On the other hand, endurance meetings retain a stable and competitive crowd. National events draw large grids and many local championships are very well supported. Traditionally, the nature of the four-stroke kart engine saw these unable to match the frantic acceleration of a two-stroke unit although an advantage in corners will usually see very little difference in overall lap times between the two kart types. Furthermore, a recent influx of powerful high-performance four-stroke engines from leading two-stroke manufacturers has caught the attention of many within the karting community and look set to establish themselves as popular options.

Classes

Newcomers to karting will often find the number of different classes bewildering. They should take comfort from the fact many already within the community are not necessarily any the wiser. Generally, categories are split between two-stroke, four-stroke and gearbox alternatives, and further segregated by age restrictions (cadet, junior or senior) and engine type (often from the same manufacturer). The following are the main MSA-

recognised classes in the UK, along with a number of leading and officially sanctioned international series. Of course, considerably more options exist outside of this circle – such as local club championships or county-wide competitions – and the racing can be just as much fun, as well as considerably cheaper. But anyone looking to get serious about karting should eventually find themselves racing in one of the classes detailed here.

UK kart classes

Bambino class

Age: 6-8th birthday

Engine: 50cc Comer engine

A new class introduced in 2010 following a surge of interest in karting in the UK due in part, no doubt, to the F1 successes of Jenson Button and Lewis Hamilton, Bambino karting enables boys and girls aged six to the day of their eighth birthday to get behind the wheel of a mean, lean, racing machine – relatively speaking, naturally. Given the young ages involved, the karts run 50cc engines limited to 3bhp and the competition takes place in the form of individual time trials, with drivers rewarded according to how they perform compared with the track's target time (set by an experienced Cadet driver). There is no racing allowed between competitors and youngsters are only permitted to take to the track if they hold an MSA kart clubman licence (available on the day or from the MSA, and free for first time applicants under the age of 16) and following an appraisal by an ARKS (Association of Racing Kart Schools – see Appendix 2) instructor.

ABOVE Boys and girls as young as six can now take to the track and show off their potential, thanks to the Bambino class. Similar classes for budding racing stars exist around the world (eg, Kids Kart in the USA or Midgets in Australia). *(Chris Walker)*

Cadet classes

The first taste of wheel-to-wheel competition young karters are allowed to have is in one of the Cadet classes, where they can remain until the end of the year of their 13th or 14th birthday (although it is possible to switch to certain Junior classes from the age of 11 – dependant on weight and height). The Comer, Honda and WTP Cadet classes are allowed to race together, all run a mini-sized kart (with prices controlled by an agreed maximum), engines with a centrifugal clutch and recoil pull cord (or electric start), and can reach speeds of around 50mph.

Comer Cadet

Age: 8-13th birthday

Engine: 60cc sealed two-stroke Comer engine

Very popular series for budding F1 champions which is run by most clubs. The sealed engine unit requires rebuilds to be carried out by approved service agents (and controls costs/performance).

BELOW For most youngsters getting into karting, the Comer Cadet class represents their first experience of wheel-to-wheel action. *(Author)*

Honda Cadet

Age: 8-13th birthday

Engine: Honda GX160 four-stroke engine

Similar to the Comer class but featuring a four-stroke Honda engine, meaning longer running times between rebuilds and therefore significantly lower running costs.

WTP Cadet

Age: 8-13th birthday

Engine: 60cc two-stroke engine with electric push-button start

Another starter class for youngsters, utilising an alternative model of 60cc two-stroke power complete with electric start. Not as popular as the other Cadet classes.

Super Cadet

Age: 11-14th birthday

Engine: 60cc two-stroke engine with electric start

Introduced in 2011 as an intermediate step between the existing Cadet and Junior classes as a way to address concerns regarding smaller young racers stepping into adult-sized kart classes too early. Maximum kart weight without driver is 80kg, while minimum with driver is 115kg. An experienced Cadet may enter the class on or after their tenth birthday.

Juniors classes

The next step for future F1 champions, the Juniors classes enjoy nationwide support, healthy grids and great, close-fought competition at speeds between 55mph to 75mph, depending on class. Formula TKM ruled the UK kart circuits for almost two decades but has now been overtaken by the Rotax Max categories, which offer near-identical performance to traditional 100cc engines but with fewer inconveniences. Conversely, Rotax Max typically demands more experience from drivers and is more expensive to begin with – although the 125cc water-cooled TAG engines used run for longer between rebuilds (limited revs ensure rebuild intervals of around 25 hours, a revolution in two-stroke karting), meaning running costs can be lower than TKM. That said, TKM has retained great support in certain parts of the country so, as ever, it's best to check what class is run at your local club.

Mini Max 11+

Age: 11-17th birthday

Engine: Restricted 125cc two-stroke Rotax Max TAG engine

The entry-level class for Rotax Max, Mini Max utilises a heavily restricted 125cc Rotax Max unit. As with all Rotax Max engines, these are sealed in an attempt to ensure a level playing field and come with a logbook detailing their service history.

LEFT Formula TKM's power unit is just one of the higher-profile examples of the new generation of four-stroke engines emerging from leading manufacturers. *(Author)*

Junior Max

Age: 13-17th birthday

Engine: 125cc two-stroke Rotax Max TAG engine

Removing the restrictor from a Mini Max kart converts it into a Junior Max and with this comes a considerable increase in speed (around 70mph). As one of the most powerful Juniors classes in the UK, this is not an advisable route for newcomers to the sport (Mini Max offers a considerably more gradual introduction to the world of 125cc two-stroke kart racing).

Junior TKM 11+

Age: 11-17th birthday

Engine: Restricted TKM BT82 100cc two-stroke engine

A once very popular class that has kept a decent presence in clubs across the UK but which is arguably under threat from the success of its Rotax Max counterpart. Junior TKM engines are restricted to limit the power and have a TAG option.

KF3

Age: 13-17th birthday

Engine: 125cc water-cooled two-stroke TAG engine

Also raced at international level, the KF3 class has increasingly shown up at championship events in the UK. As with Junior Max, this is a class for experienced karters only.

Seniors classes

As you might expect, these are more powerful versions of the Juniors classes for competitors aged 16 and over, with top speeds approaching 85mph. Again, Rotax Max is the most widely supported category in the UK, with TKM Extreme's popularity now mostly restricted to specific areas. However, more disciplines outside of these two exist (Formula TKM runs a promising senior four-stroke class, for instance), not least the presence of premier categories such as KF1 and KF2 – which replace past classes Formula A and ICA – at major championships like the Super One series (see International classes for more details).

TKM Extreme

Age: 16 years+

Engine: TKM BT82 115cc two-stroke engine with TAG option

Once hugely popular, TKM Extreme has seen its widespread presence significantly reduced by the arrival of the 125cc TAG classes. Nevertheless, it has kept a regional and loyal following in the UK – you may well find that it's the most common series run at your local club. It remains a very economical senior class, with cost control very much at the heart of the series' philosophy.

Gearbox classes

This is where you'll find the pinnacle of kart racing, with the highest speeds and power reserved for the geared classes. They come in a variety of flavours featuring four-wheel braking, up to seven-speed engines and, in Superkart form, are capable of more than 150mph. Offering traditional single-seater racing car handling and acceleration, these machines are for very experienced karters only. Gearbox classes are the only karts eligible to run on long circuits such as Silverstone, and use a hand or foot clutch (usually only relied upon for standing starts) in addition to the standard brake and throttle pedals.

ICC UK
Age: 16 years+
Engine: 125cc water-cooled six-speed engine
Effectively the UK version of KZ2 (see International classes) and regarded as the entry-level gearbox class, ICC is also the most popular and probably the most economical category in this class. But don't let that fool you: with 0-60mph in less than four seconds and a 90mph top speed (120mph on long circuits), this is no place for beginners or thin wallets. (As ever, other gearbox classes such as KZ1 – detailed in International classes – are also run at national-level championships.)

ABOVE Unarguably the leading senior class – in the UK, at least – Rotax Max currently enjoys great support thanks in no small part to its revolutionary two-stroke engines. *(Author)*

Rotax Max
Age: 16 years+
Engine: 125cc two-stroke Rotax Max TAG engine
With the full power of the 125cc Rotax Max engine unleashed, this is a serious and highly competitive series for seasoned karters. Although the sealed engines prevent illegal tuning, and maintenance tends to be lower than most 100cc classes, costs in Rotax Max can be high.

RIGHT Hardly the realm of the beginner, Superkarts represent the ultimate in karting performance, and while not the focus of this book, their extreme nature nevertheless guarantees them a fleeting inclusion. *(Chris Walker)*

250 National

Age: 16 years+ (17 years+ for long circuit)

Engine: 250cc single-cylinder motocross engine

The most powerful short circuit class, capable of 100mph (140mph on long circuits) and relying on established five-speed motorcross engines. A relatively popular class, with karts sporting full-width nosecones and rear wings due to their performance.

210 National

Age: 16 years+

Engine: 197cc Viliers air-cooled engine

A classic category that uses the Viliers 197cc engine (or replicas) and is administered by the drivers themselves through the 210 Challenge group.

Superkarts

Age: 17 years+

Engine: 250cc twin-cylinder six-speed engine

The fastest – and most intimidating – of the gearbox classes, able to reach speeds close to 160mph due to 250cc twin-cylinder engines outputting around 90bhp. Their extreme nature ensures they're only used on long (full-size) motor racing circuits, where they enjoy healthy grids.

USA kart classes

As you might imagine with a territory as expansive as the USA, there are enough kart race series and engine types supported throughout this vast nation to fill this book with. In the interest of covering a wide selection while leaving a little space for the other chapters, only the main WKA national series (and associated classes) are briefly listed to give an overview of the range of kart racing in North America.

Manufacturer's Cup Series

A five-race national championship on sprint-style road courses for two-stroke powered karts, with competitors ranging from five to over 50 years of age.

Kid Kart

Age: 5-7 years

Engine: Restricted 50cc Comer

Cadet Sportsman 1 and 2

Age: 8-12 years

Engine: Restricted 80cc two-stroke Comer K-80

Komet Sportsman

Age: 8-12 years

Engine: Restricted HPV Komet Piston Port two-stroke

Yamaha Sportsman Lite and Heavy

Age: 8-12 years

Engine: Restricted two-stroke Yamaha

Komet Junior Lite and Heavy

Age: 12-15 years

Engine: HPV Komet Piston Port two-stroke

Yamaha Junior Lite and Heavy

Age: 12-15 years

Engine: Two-stroke Yamaha

Komet Lite and Heavy

Age: 15-35

Engine: HPV Komet Piston Port two-stroke

Yamaha Supercan Lite and Heavy

Age: 15-35

Engine: Two-stroke Yamaha

TAG

Age: 15-35

Engine: BM Jaguar, Cheetah SQ 125, Comer K365, Easykart, Morori Seven, Parilla Leopard, Rotax FR 125, Sonik TX, Sonik VX, Vortex Rok, Vortex Rok TT, PRD Fire Ball

Yamaha Masters

Age: 35 years+

Engine: Two-stroke Yamaha

TAG Masters

Age: 35 years+

Engine: As per TAG class

Gold Cup Series

Four-race national rounds for four-stroke karts on sprint-style circuits and with competitors aged between five and 60-plus.

Kid Kart

Age: 5-7 years

Engine: Restricted 50cc Comer

Sportsman 1 Lite and Heavy

Age: 8-10 years

Engine: Briggs & Stratton Stock Animal

Sportsman 2 Lite and Heavy

Age: 10-12 years

Engine: Briggs & Stratton Stock Animal

Restricted Junior

Age: 12-15 years

Engine: Briggs & Stratton Stock Animal

Junior Lite, Medium and Heavy

Age: 12-15 years

Engine: Briggs & Stratton Stock Animal

Animal Lite, Medium and Heavy

Age: 15 years+

Engine: Briggs & Stratton Stock Animal

Animal Modified Medium and Heavy

Age: 15 years+

Engine: Briggs & Stratton Modified Animal

Masters Medium and Heavy

Age: 35 years+

Engine: Briggs & Stratton Stock Animal

National Road Race Series – Laydown and Sprint Sit-up classes

Formerly Enduro Series, this eight- or nine-round national series is held at some of America's most famous road tracks such as Daytona International Speedway and Road America. Laydown-enduro and sprint-enduro karts are built specifically for endurance-style road racing. The Road Race events are timed, with sprint-enduro rounds lasting 30 minutes and laydown-enduro finishing after 45 minutes.

Junior Enduro Lite and Heavy (Laydown)

Age: 12-15 years

Engine: Yamaha engine only

Piston Port Can Lite, Medium and Heavy (Laydown)

Age: 15 years+

Engine: Yamaha, ARC Comer, PRD PK 100

100cc Pipe Medium and Heavy (Laydown)

Age: 16 years+

Engine: Yamaha KT100, ARC Comer P-50, ARC Comer P-51, PRD RK100, Parilla PV-92, Komet K-71, TKM BT81, PRC PP-100, DAP T-50, HPV 100

Yamaha Sportsman Medium and Heavy (Laydown)

Age: 16 years+

Engine: Yamaha KT100

100cc Controlled (Laydown)

Age: 16 years+

Engine: 100cc Yamaha, Piston Port, ICA Reed engines

Unlimited Final 1 and 2 (Laydown)

Age: 18 years+

Engine: 250cc gearbox twin-cylinder, 250cc gearbox single-cylinder, 100-450cc single cylinder (100cc and 135cc allowed as twin-engine configuration)

Formula 100 1 and 2 (Laydown)

Age: 16 years+

Engine: 100-135cc open, Comer MIK351L, CRG S10-T1, DAP T85, Ital ML21, Jako 2LA, Parilla Reed Jet, CR TSL95 & TSL98, Rotax R-100 VM-E

Formula 125 (Laydown)

Age: 18 years+

Engine: 125cc gearbox, B Limited, or Open

Animal Junior Sprint Lite and Heavy

Age: 12-15 years

Engine: Briggs & Stratton Animal

Junior Sprint Lite and Heavy

Age: 12-15 years

Engine: Yamaha, ARC Comer, PRD RK100

WKA Sprint 1 and 2

Age: 16 years+

Engine: Yamaha KT100S, ARC Comer, PRD RK100

CIK 125 Shifter 1 and 2

Age: 18 years+

Engine: 125cc Honda CR Reed, Kawasaki KX Reed, Suzuki RM Reed, Yamaha YX Reed, Gilera 125cc and TM Motocross

SPEC 125 TAG 1 and 2
Age: 16 years+
Engine: BM Jaguar, Easykart 125, Parilla Leopard, Rotax, Sonik VX125

TAG 1 and 2
Age: 16 years+
Engine: BM Jaguar, Cheetah SQ125, Comer K365, Easykart, Motori Seven, Stock Parilla Leopard, Ported Parilla Leopard, PRD Fire Ball, Rotax FR 125, Sonik TX 125, Sonik TX, Vortex Rok, Vortex Rok TT

Stock Honda 1 and 2
Age: 18 years+
Engine: Honda CR125 RX

Speedway Pavement Series

National tour comprising five races with 20 classes powered by four-stroke engines (all Briggs & Stratton Stock Animal units, with the exception of the Kid Kart classes which use Subaru Robin and Comer C-50/C-51) and run on asphalt ovals across the Northeast, Midwest and South.

Speedway Dirt Series

A five-race Southeast championship and the only WKA series that takes place on dirt, with most classes powered by Briggs & Stratton four-stroke engines and competitors ranging in age from five to 60-plus.

Additional series

Other popular kart classes in North America include series often found internationally, such as Rotax Mini Max, KF3, KF2, KZ2 and Superkarts.

International kart classes

The top-level international championships are sanctioned by the CIK-FIA and are also widely run at national and continental level. The main categories are highlighted below and form the career path for those looking to stay in karting professionally or move on to other categories of motorsport.

KF3

Age: 12-15 years

Engine: KF 125cc water-cooled two-stroke TAG engine

Junior Intercontinental A (JICA), now known as KF3, is similar in essence to the other KF series but aimed at a younger age group. As such, engines are limited to 14,000rpm but the talent certainly isn't – this is one of the highest classes of karting, with national, continental and world-level championships, as well as premier events such as the yearly Junior Monaco Kart Cup.

KF2

Age: 15 years+

Engine: KF 125cc water-cooled two-stroke TAG engine

Formerly Intercontinental A (ICA), KF2 may look deceptively similar to KF1 on paper, but subtle differences exist. The engine is the same 125cc water-cooled two-stroke TAG unit with clutch, but KF2 karts are limited to 15,000rpm and boast less bottom end grunt. They're no slouches, though, and are run at national, continental and world level. Drivers must finish in the top 34 in KF2 before they are allowed to take part in KF1.

KF1

Age: 15 years+

Engine: KF 125cc water-cooled two-stroke TAG engine

Previously known as Formula A, KF1 has since 2007 used 125cc TAG engines limited to 16,000rpm (in order to extend engine life) which can propel the chassis they're attached to at speeds up to 85mph. KF1 represents the top level of karting, with European and world championships bringing together the sport's very best talent but the costs can be astronomical.

KZ2

Age: 15 years+

Engine: 125cc water-cooled six-speed engine

Intercontinental C (ICC) is now KZ2 and similar in terms of technical regulations to its slightly bigger brother, KZ1. The main differences affect tyre options (medium for KZ2, soft for KZ1) and the use of a hand-operated mechanical gearbox (KZ1 gearboxes can be electromechanical). KZ2 events are particularly popular in the USA, although Europe sees considerable support for the class, too.

KZ1

Age: 15 years+

Engine: 125cc water-cooled six-speed engine

Known previously as Super ICC, the six-speed KZ1 karts are heavier than direct drive karts and require a different approach with regards to driving technique. KZ1 is raced at national, continental and world level.

Superkart

Age: 17 years+

Engine: 250cc twin-cylinder six-speed engine

No different to the Superkart class in the UK (see previously), the world's fastest karts enjoy support around the globe from a competitive crowd of top class drivers hooked on this category's awesome cornering and braking ability.

BELOW Working your way up to international level karting – such as KZ2 – will take time, talent and tonnes of money. But the beauty of karting is that you can have a blast with just about any category. *(Chris Walker)*

Choosing a kart class

Despite the intimidating range of karting classes available, your options are soon reduced once you approach things systematically. As a beginner, gearbox classes are out of the question, and if you're 16 and above, that also rules out the Cadet and Junior options.

For most people, it's then usually a case of finding out what is being raced at their local track. If the options are severely limited or unsuitable due to the level of your ability, consider neighbouring clubs. Don't be put off by a class that only races at one circuit if you're planning to use it as a learning exercise but with time you may want to be racing at various tracks around the country. If this is something you're prepared to do from the start then obviously extend your search to include clubs that are farther away. Consider the fact this may limit your ability to test or practice regularly, however.

The popularity of karting classes can alter remarkably quickly, so before committing to one, do a little research online (through karting news sites, forums and track websites) and read karting magazines to get an idea of how healthy a particular series is looking. Remember that fewer numbers has an impact on the second-hand market, as well as the amount of clubs at which you will be able to race your chosen kart.

Finally, if it's all looking a little bleak in terms of options, don't despair. Having to join a class that demands a little more experience than you may currently have isn't the end of the world. You're unlikely to win your first meetings, true, but you may be surprised by how quickly you progress in a relatively short amount of time. Don't be afraid to put yourself in the odd challenging situation now and again – it's one of the ways humans develop their skills best and this obviously applies directly to your ability as a racing driver, too.

BELOW Clubman-level racing may lack the glamour of F1, but you will relish your first piece of silverware. *(Greg Richardson)*

2

Getting started

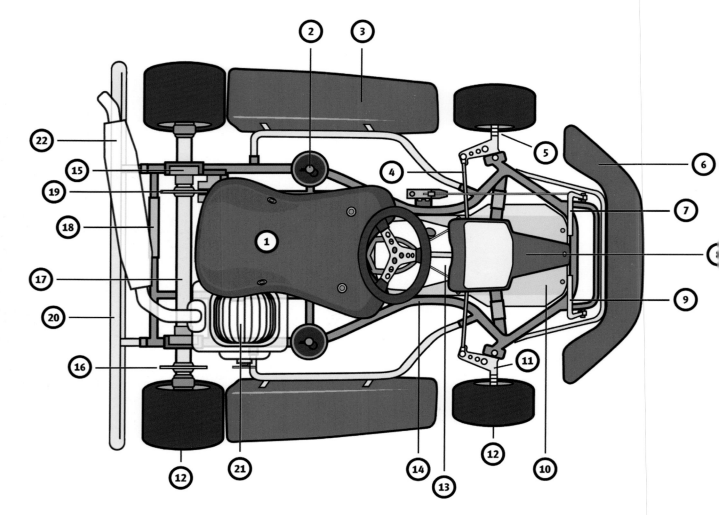

Introduction

As with any technical sport, starting out can seem a little bewildering for the novice. Karting is no exception, but it is worth realising that it is actually reasonably easy to get into and, of course, you're not expected to know everything from the moment you first sit in the kart. You're always learning in fact, but the following chapter should hopefully help in making the first steps a little less daunting.

The kart

A kart is actually a very straightforward piece of engineering, and that's part of its appeal. It is effectively little more than a chassis with a seat, a steering wheel, an engine, a braking system, four wheels fitted with tubeless racing tyres, and no suspension. For all intents and purposes, it's a single-seater racing car distilled to its core components – any simpler and it wouldn't work.

That's not to say a racing kart doesn't offer a degree of complexity when it comes to, say, set-up – it does – but it's obviously a world away from the intricacies you would face in a higher forms of motorsport such as Formula One. Having said that, the same fundamentals apply, but we'll get to that later.

An initial detailed look at a kart will reveal a multitude of nuts, bolts, cables and components, but you'll be surprised at how quickly everything becomes familiar. That is partly because nearly everything on a kart is open to scrutiny, meaning that you can usually work out a component's role simply by looking at it. Equally, it makes maintenance, repair and set-up far more straightforward.

Familiarity with your kart is obviously crucial in terms of making sure it is ready for going on the track so spend the time to get to know it. If you are in any doubt with regards to any aspect of your kart, get it checked by an experienced driver or club official before you get in and drive it.

Getting in

The correct way to get into a stationary kart is to step directly on to the seat and not the chassis or between the chassis members (which can be a sure way of braking an ankle should your kart suddenly get bumped by another kart coming into the pits as you're stepping in). Once you're standing on the seat and are facing forward, rest both hands on the back of the seat and lower yourself into it, sliding your left leg into position, followed by your right leg. Doing it the other way around could see you stepping on the accelerator first, which could be interesting if your engine is running.

To get out of a kart, simply reverse the sequence. Start by resting your hands on the back of the seat for leverage, pull your right leg up first, followed by your left leg and stand on the seat. Then simply step over the side pod and clear of the kart.

Driving position

The first thing to note is that when you're sitting in position, with your shoulders parallel with the back of the seat, your arms should be slightly bent. The seat should be snug, your back straight and you should not hunch – leaning forward affects the weight balance in a kart and can make it difficult to drive consistently. Your posture should be upright and your knees bent, even when the pedals are fully depressed. Both steering wheel and pedals can usually be adjusted in order to achieve the correct driving position. It's worth remembering that seat positioning is absolutely crucial to a kart's handling, so this should always take priority. Once the seat is in the correct place, you can then tinker with steering wheel and pedal positioning.

As for holding the steering wheel, if you look at the top drivers you'll note most of them either hold it at a 'ten-to-two' or a 'quarter-to-three' position. The former is generally accepted as the ideal position because of the leverage it enables and how this affects the chassis, although some drivers never get on with it and prefer the more symmetrical 'quarter-to-three' or 'nine-fifteen' alternative. In addition, steering wheel design and

individual kart dynamics will have an effect on which grip you should opt for.

Once in position, your hands should not move on the wheel. The steering system on a kart goes from lock to lock in just half a turn, meaning there is no need to reposition the hands, even when going around a tight hairpin.

Buying a kart

There are many kart chassis available and choosing the right one comes down to your budget and level of experience.

When starting out, there is a very strong argument against spending most of your cash on a brand-new chassis. You shouldn't be expecting to win the first races you enter and you're likely to spend a lot of your time going off the track. Therefore, ruining a costly new chassis seems like an unnecessary waste of money, particularly when you can probably buy a good second-hand chassis complete with spares such as a set of wet wheels, a stand, chains, sprockets and so on for considerably less outlay.

A decent used chassis is perfectly suited for gaining experience, which should be the focus of any new driver. Of course, buying a used kart when you're new to the sport can be a daunting prospect so, if possible, you should take an experienced karter with you as they will be better able to assess whether the chassis is damaged, or parts such as the front and rear bumper comply with current regulations, and therefore whether it is a good deal or not. While chassis are reasonably resilient, try not to buy something that has had more than one or two seasons' use.

OPPOSITE

Typical Kart layout
1   Seat
2   Ballast mounting post
    (can also be carried
    on back of seat)
3   Protective sidepod
4   Track rod
5   Spacers (used to alter
    the front track width)
6   Front bumper
7   Brake pedal
8   Nosecone
9   Throttle pedal
10 Floorplate
11 Stub axle
12 Wheel rim
13 Fuel tank
14 Chassis
15 Bearings
16 Sprocket
17 Rear axle
18 Torsion bar
19 Brake system
20 Rear bumper
21 Engine
22 Exhaust

BELOW Two-stroke karts without a clutch need to be push-started, an easy technique to learn. The trick is to be light on the throttle until the engine picks up.
(Enver Meyer)

As for the model itself, visit your local track and talk to the competitors to find out what they are racing. By keeping an eye on the race results across a variety of clubs you will also get to know what is winning, which should help narrow down your potential choices. You will find the classified ads in karting magazines, on websites and even on the notice board of your local track as good sources of equipment for sale. But do your research as some makes are not as widely supported as others, which could make finding spares and technical backing more difficult.

Consider also the type of makes your local karting dealers stock. Given the growth of internet commerce and the fact you can pretty much get any kart part online these days, this may not seem crucial, but having their experience and advice on-hand can be invaluable and more than worth the extra it's likely to cost purchasing from a retailer rather than an online store.

Once you've progressed to a level where buying a new chassis is necessary, you will need to test drive those on your shortlist to get an idea of how well they suit your driving style. Kart chassis may look similar but the difference in handling characteristics can be surprising, to the point where some drivers simply won't get on with a particular design. Again, the more experience you have, the easier it will become to spot these differences. Obviously, bear in mind that settings will also have a significant effect when it comes to maximising your potential – as with karting in general, the chassis is just one component of the overall package.

Safety equipment and kart wear

You can't go racing without the appropriate mandatory safety gear, and you wouldn't want to anyway. While karting is statistically far safer than many other sports, there is inherent danger in zooming around a track at high speeds, surrounded by other karts doing the exact same thing. Common sense prevents many incidents but there are some you won't be able to avoid. For those instances, wearing the following items is crucial.

Helmet (compulsory)

A good-quality full-face helmet or lid should be the very first item on your list of racing equipment. Prices can vary considerably, but it is worth buying the best lid your budget will allow. Don't be tempted to buy a cheaper motorcycle model, for instance – to be approved for MSA events, a kart helmet must adhere to specific safety standards that do not necessarily apply to everyday road-use models. The current requirements are listed in the *MSA Competitor's Yearbook* that UK drivers receive when applying for a licence (see below) but any reputable karting or motorsport retailer will be able to ensure you purchase the appropriate helmet.

As important as buying an approved helmet, is getting one that is the correct size. A lid should fit snugly and the first time you put it on it will feel way too small, almost as though you'll never get your head in it, but you soon get used to it. Again, a retailer will help but as a rough guide if you can just catch the inside of your cheeks with your teeth as you open and close your mouth and the lid doesn't feel loose on your head then it's probably as close-fitting as it should be – any smaller and you'll probably end up with a headache after prolonged use.

Finally, look after it. Helmets are expensive and are constructed in a way as to absorb impact once – so even dropping it on a hard surface is enough to severely affect its structure, meaning it would no longer protect you in the event of a crash. If you're in any doubt over the status of your lid, nearly all manufacturers will perform a structural integrity assessment provided you send them the helmet for inspection. So take care when carrying it around the paddock (or where you place it in your pit area – at ground level is always best), invest in a padded helmet bag for transit, clean it after every race, and store it away safely when not in use.

When you do use it, always make sure it is properly strapped every time you get in the kart.

www.araihelmet-europe.com

Race suit (compulsory)

There are many styles of kart suits from many manufacturers, offering anything from the most basic cover to multi-layered, fully padded material incorporating body protection panels. Whichever type you opt for, it will need to meet CIK (the specialised karting commission of the FIA, motorsport's world governing body) regulations, meaning that it offers a specified level of safety, such as abrasion resistance. Kart suits do not need to be fireproof.

When buying a race suit, ensure that it fits comfortably and does not restrict movement, particularly around the arms and shoulders (many suits include stretch panels in these areas). It should also be long enough to cover your wrists and ankles when in a sitting position. Remember that during winter racing you may be wearing thicker inner clothing than during the summer months, so allow for that provision.

A race suit will easily last several seasons provided you look after it. Allow it to air after each meeting and washing it regularly to remove oil, grease and petrol will also help prolong its life.

Finally, remember to keep it zipped up while you're out on the track. Getting black flagged because you forgot to do up your suit won't make you feel too clever about yourself.

Gloves (compulsory)

Gloves need to be tight fitting with decent flexibility to enable a good feel of the steering wheel while also offering appropriate protection. Many are specifically tailored for karting and whichever you choose (consider one with extended elasticated wrist cover), it is important to keep them clean. Getting oil or grease on either the inside or outside of gloves will reduce the grip level on the steering wheel, which is vital for control, so avoid the common mistake of working on the kart with them – invest in a pair of mechanic's gloves instead. It is also a good idea to keep a spare pair of driving gloves in your kit bag should you rip your current pair during practice or qualifying, as you could be excluded from taking part in any further of the day's events if they are found to be inadequate for racing.

Boots (compulsory)

Race boots have deliberately thin narrow soles to ensure flexibility, which in turn means a driver has the best pedal sensitivity, crucial for kart control. Whether you go for a high or low-cut style, padded ankle cover is essential to protect against impact (and a regulatory requirement), while a top Velcro strap can be useful in terms of keeping laces from getting caught on anything that could result in a serious incident.

Neck brace

After the above four purchases, the next vital item is a neck brace. You may not see many drivers wearing them as they are not compulsory, even in the top series, but a chat with an experienced racer who will no doubt have witnessed their fair share of accidents where unprotected drivers ended up taking a quick trip to the local hospital or, worse, in a wheelchair, would probably convince them to do so.

A decent neck brace works by restricting head movement during an impact, meaning the risk of a serious neck injury is reduced. Another potential injury during high-velocity frontal crashes is a broken collar bone resulting from the impact of the bottom of the helmet as the driver's head is suddenly thrust sideways – in these cases, the padding from a neck brace almost certainly prevents this from happening.

This isn't to say you'll be dicing with death whenever you get on the track. Far from it. The vast majority of kart meetings take place without serious incidents, and even dramatic-looking crashes will often cause little more than some nasty looking bruises. However, motorsport, by its very nature, can be dangerous. Accidents are unpredictable and while you cannot prepare for every eventuality, it obviously makes absolute sense to reduce the risk as much as possible. When you consider that a neck brace is cheap, takes seconds to put on or take off, is extremely light, and could prevent you from spending the rest of your life as a spectator of motorsport rather than as a competitor, there is really no argument against using one.

Rib protector

Another recommended, although not mandatory, piece of safety equipment is a rib protector. Cracking a rib can be surprisingly easy – drivers have done so as a result of the jolt caused by simply clipping a kerb a little too enthusiastically, which is transferred through the side of the seat – and aside from being extremely painful, the fact it takes between six to eight weeks to heal means you'll miss race meetings while you're recuperating.

Many of the models available on the market are little more than flimsy pieces of thin foam that will do little to protect you in a serious impact. However, some good solid types exist which offer excellent protective qualities. It is important to choose one that allows good adjustability to ensure it is in the correct position without interfering with your movement, as well as allowing the option of wearing it on the outside of the suit, should you find that is your preference.

Wetsuit

Something of an essential item in the UK, particularly if you plan on doing endurance racing, a karting wetsuit keeps you dry when the heavens open, which aside from helping prevent a possible cold, also gives you a significant advantage in terms of not letting the rain affect your racing ability (as discussed in Chapter 5). Many examples are made far more cheaply than their inflated prices would suggest and rip easily or are designed in such a way as to do little to prevent water from coming into contact with your race suit.

Some of the more expensive alternatives are good but consider, too, a motorbike wetsuit – they are usually considerably cheaper yet better made and feature more intelligent design while still keeping the flexibility you need for karting. Alternatively, outdoor specialist stores can offer a good range of waterproof wear that can work just as effectively. Wetsuits don't have to meet CIK regulations so the choice is open (make sure the model you choose does not feature a rain hood, though, as you may not be allowed to race with it).

Balaclava

Not mandatory for karting, but good to keep your helmet environment a little more hygienic and by tucking it into your race suit it also offers a little extra protection for your neck (and keeps it warmer during winter races).

Underwear

There is no set rule, here. You can buy specific karting underwear which has been especially designed to keep you cooler and is certainly comfortable but many drivers opt for a light, snug T-shirt and don't seem to suffer adversely. Keeping your temperature regulated is important because it can affect your driving, but as long as you find a solution that works for you and doesn't impede your performance, don't worry too much about what everyone else is wearing.

One obvious exception to the rule of doing everything to keep your temperature low is during winter months, when full thermal wear can make a significant difference, particularly in terms of keeping your legs and, crucially, your feet warm. Cold feet inevitably mean you lose sensitivity, so you won't be able to feel the pedals properly and your lap times are likely to suffer.

Knee and elbow pads

Knees are particularly vulnerable during races and can take a bit of a battering against the fuel tank/steering column while elbows can also suffer depending on your driving style. Protective pads can help but many drivers find the elastic on them too tight and prefer to go without. If you can get past this, they are certainly a recommended addition for long endurance events requiring you to do several stints.

Other equipment

While by no means an exhaustive list, the following are some of the most common items you will need to go karting regularly.

Tools

The type of tools you require are detailed in Chapter 9 but at this stage, it shouldn't come as a shock to learn that you need a decent amount of kit for karting. Thankfully, much is likely to be found in the average household toolbox but others are specific to the sport, while some will need duplicating in order to maximise efficiency.

While it is not necessary to turn up at your first race meeting with a complete set (the friendly atmosphere of local karting means it is not uncommon to be able to borrow another team's tools, certainly when starting out), it is important to ensure the tools you do buy are of the best quality you can afford. Cheaply made tools are a bad investment, will ruin your equipment and generally make your track life more difficult. If looked after properly, there's no reason decent tools won't last many, many years – if you consider the long term picture, the initial additional outlay required to purchase them will seem far more reasonable.

Transport

Perhaps the most immediate and cost-effective way to transport your kart and equipment to the race track is to use the family car, provided it is suited to the task. With the wheels off, many karts will fit into the back of the average estate model, but this should only be considered as a short-term solution.

A more practical approach is to opt for a trailer. Generic models are relatively inexpensive and can be adapted to suit your needs without too much effort although if your budget allows it, a better option would be to invest in a model specifically suited to karting. These are usually walk-in box

BELOW A dedicated team van doesn't have to be very expensive and is perfect for the job. *(Enver Meyer)*

trailer types, offer better security and feature a tailored interior designed to take your kart (often without needing to remove its wheels), spare tyres, and all other associated equipment.

Once you become more serious about the sport, you may want to consider the advantages offered the use of a dedicated van. For some, it may be possible to borrow or use a van from work for racing at the weekend. If this doesn't apply to you, don't worry because cheap second-hand vans in good condition aren't hard to find. As with trailers, vans come in all shapes and sizes but deliver a level of versatility that trailers cannot match. Obviously most of that is due to the extra amount of space you get in a van, meaning you're able to store your equipment in such a way that doesn't require the entire removal of the contents in order to get to a spare part, for instance, therefore

helping with the organisational side of things and saving you time at the track.

Most teams refurbish the inside of their van so as to maximise both the utility and space of the interior (eg so there is space for multiple chassis, a crucial consideration given it is the most space-demanding item), and on bigger models it is not unusual to find a built-in compartment that incorporates basic living quarters, which are ideal for saving on accommodation fees when travelling to distant circuits.

Stands

You can't work on a kart properly if it is sitting on the ground. A kart stand is essential in order to carry out maintenance or set-up work and also makes transporting your kart around the paddock a breeze. Models with large inflatable tyres make it

BELOW A kart stand is essential to get yourself easily around the paddock and for when working on the kart. *(Darren Bourne)*

easier to negotiate the cracked, uneven surface of some clubs' paddock area. Solo competitors should consider a unit specifically designed to enable a single individual to set the kart on the ground without the need for assistance from a second person.

Transponder

Most kart clubs will require teams to own their own transponder (normally an AMB TranX-160) to enable computer timing and lap scoring to be made. Some clubs may also hire these out on a per event basis but you should find this out before turning up on race day.

Stopwatch

Of primary value for the team manager, a stopwatch can do more than just enable those standing in the pits to record your lap times. It is also crucial for working out gaps to other drivers, as well as keeping an eye on the competition's lap times, particularly during testing and practice sessions when times are not necessarily displayed on the official timing screen. Choose a motorsport-specific model featuring multiple lap counting ability and other useful features that cheap, standard stopwatches rarely include.

Pit board

An essential item, this enables communication with a driver while they are out on the track, transmitting information such as position, the gap to other drivers, the remaining number of laps, pit stops and more. Ready-made solutions are available but, equally, a home-made pit board can function just as effectively and is obviously a lot cheaper. Even if you rely on radio communication with your driver, a

pit board should form part of your equipment and would become the backup form or communication in case of problems with the radio units.

Radio communication

Another way of communicating with the driver that is becoming increasingly popular, particularly for endurance races, is by radio. The cheapest option is to purchase a set of walkie-talkies and incorporate a motorbike speaker and microphone kit into the driver's helmet, although this solution may prove unfeasible to cope with the noise of a two-stroke engine. However, dedicated karting communication solutions exist, albeit at a price.

Awning

The last thing you want when working on your kart in between rounds is to be doing this in the rain. You'll rush your work, possibly make mistakes, get frustrated, wet and cold. Hardly the right mental state from which to then go on and race. Awnings aren't cheap but will make a massive difference to the quality of your race day. Go for the biggest you can afford (within reason) and consider a model that comes with removable side panels to really keep the weather out and the temperature up when needed. Remember to weigh it down (filling old kart tyres with cement and an embedded iron hook from which to tie a harness is an easy and cheap solution), even during calm days. The sight of an awning caught by a sudden gust and tumbling down the paddock or the car park (causing considerable cosmetic damage to any vehicles in its path), is not as uncommon as you'd think.

ABOVE An awning makes a crucial difference to the quality of trackside life.
(Enver Meyer)

RIGHT Most lap
counters do much more
than simply keep a
record of your times.
(Author)

Lap timer

A digital timing unit is expensive but eventually vital
to keep track of your lap times as well as
determining whether changes in set-up have made
you faster or slower (and where). Most work by
picking up magnetic strips that are already placed
at various intervals on a race track and displaying
your lap or section time accordingly. Depending on
the model, you can also get information detailing
engine revs, overall race time (for endurance),
temperature readings (water, oil, cylinder and
exhaust), and speed while some even feature a
g-force meter as well as the ability to extract the
data on to a PC for you to analyse after a race or
test session. If you're planning on entering late
evening or night-time races, consider a unit offering
a backlit display.

Fire extinguisher

For MSA events, every competitor is required to
carry a fire extinguisher in their car or van. The
standard and size rating should be detailed in the
MSA Competitor's Yearbook.

First aid kit

It is not uncommon to suffer small cuts or scrapes
from working on a kart, particularly when you first
start out. As you get familiar with the techniques

and using the required tools these will become
less regular. All MSA licensed events include a
paramedic and ambulance, but for minor injuries,
carrying a small first aid kit with you will do the job
adequately.

Consumables

Consumables in karting can obviously refer to oil,
chains and tyres, but in this particular instance it
refers to food. You'd be surprised how many
drivers forget to take nourishment and drink to their
first meeting, but it is absolutely crucial to keep
your energy and hydration levels up during race
day. At many circuits, the facilities will include a
catering van or perhaps even a dedicated cafeteria,
but at others you can find yourself in the middle of
a field with nothing but a load of kart teams and a
handful of marshals for company. Ensuring you
have the appropriate amount and right kind of food
and drink with you to get through a demanding day
of karting is obviously vital.

Race licence

If you plan on racing at officially recognised events,
you will need a racing licence. In fact, at some
circuits, even testing requires you to hold the

appropriate licence so it makes sense to obtain this as soon as you can. Most people won't find it any trouble to obtain their licence, which is in effect an introductory course to kart driving and making sure that you understand the sport's rules, such as the meaning of the marshals' flags. In the UK, you'll need an MSA racing licence.

Application form

Contact the MSA or your local ARKS circuit (you'll find contact details for both organisations in Appendix 2) and purchase a Start Karting pack. This includes a video giving a brief overview of karting in the UK and details of what to do in order to get your licence, as well as a copy of the *MSA Competitor's Yearbook* (often referred to as the 'Blue Book') and the *MSA Kart Race Yearbook* ('Gold Book') detailing all of the sport's regulations. You will need to know the sections relating to karting in order to pass the test for your licence, the application form for which you'll also find in the pack.

There are certain exemptions to the test, and these affect individuals who may have previously held certain kart, racing or foreign licences, or for those requiring a kart endurance licence. If this applies to you, you may not need to take the test.

Medical

You will need to book an appointment with your doctor for a race licence medical. This examination is not free and covers general areas such as your heart and cardiovascular system, eyesight, blood pressure and basic neurological responses (reflexes), amongst others. Its function is to determine whether you have any conditions that may prevent you from safely undertaking an activity such as racing. Remember to take your licence application form along as your doctor will have a section to fill in and sign at the end of the examination.

Test

If you require a test, you may now book one at your local ARKS circuit (some other circuits may also be approved for testing purposes). The test is divided into two parts, with one covering driving ability (karts are provided in most cases although expect to incur an extra charge for this service) and the other focusing on your knowledge of the regulations via a multiple-choice questionnaire. If you fail either section, it can be retaken for an extra fee (in addition to the original cost of the test). Drivers who don't feel ready can obviously gain experience through practice sessions at their local track before applying for their test.

Getting the licence

Once you've passed your test, send off your application form to the MSA, along with the necessary final payment, in order to obtain your licence. This usually takes 15 days, although express services are available for an additional charge.

Join a club

When you have your licence you can finally enter your first race. You will need to join an officially recognised kart club in order to enter race meetings and club championships. You can be a member of any number of kart clubs.

BELOW Once you have your MSA race licence, you can start racing straight away.
(Enver Meyer)

Flags

Flags are the only way marshals – who are positioned at various points around the track – communicate with you while you're whizzing around the circuit. They are therefore not only essential but mandatory, too, meaning that if you ignore them you should expect to have a chat with the Clerk of the Course and suffer potential penalties. Amongst other things, they are there to alert you of potential danger and it is therefore crucial that you understand their meaning before you're let loose on a circuit. Even circuits running non-licensed meetings use flags although there may be slight differences in their usage so it is therefore important to pay attention during the driver's briefing. The following are the flags used in karting, along with their official meaning.

National flag

 In cases where the starting signal lights fail, the national flag can be used to start the race. For a rolling start, start at the moment the flag is raised; for standing starts, start when the flag is dropped.

Green

A green flag indicates the road ahead is clear and you can carry on racing. They're usually seen at a marshal post once you've cleared a danger area controlled by yellow flags (if localised yellow) or at the start/finish line if the full course yellow status has ended. Either way, it means you can resume overtaking and full race speed. Green flags can also be used to signify the start of a formation lap.

Green/yellow chevron

This indicates a false start and is used in karting only. Racing should cease and once the grid is reformed the race can then be restarted.

Yellow

Yellow flags warn of danger – there has been an incident and there may be a kart, driver or marshal stationary on or near the track. When the flag is shown stationary, you should slow down to a speed at which you have full control of the kart and you are not allowed to overtake. If waved, there is great danger ahead. You should slow down considerably and be prepared to deviate from the racing line, take avoiding action or even stop. Again, no overtaking is allowed (this restriction remains in place until you see a green flag, signifying the end of the cautionary section). If you happen to overtake under a yellow and realise your mistake, many race series won't penalise you as long as you wave the passed car back into its original position as soon as possible.

Sometimes a yellow and black quartered flag is used during short circuit meetings to indicate to the drivers to slow down and not overtake although most tracks opt for a plain yellow flag to achieve the same effect. Depending on the circuit and severity of the incident, yellow flags are either used as localised warnings or extend over the full course (in which case all marshal posts will display the flags and/or be supplemented by flashing yellow lights).

Yellow/red

A cautionary flag, warning of slippery conditions. If stationary, the track ahead is slippery; if waved, a slippery surface is imminent.

Red

A red flag indicates the race has been stopped – this

can be due to a serious incident, the presence of a stationary kart in a precarious position, or something such as undrivable or dangerous weather conditions. You should immediately cease racing, slow right down and be prepared to stop on the track, although more often than not you will be directed by the marshals back to the pits or the start/finish line.

Blue

When held, the blue flag indicates that another competitor is following close behind. When waved, it indicates another competitor is trying to overtake. These are usually shown to backmarkers when the competitor behind them is a frontrunner whose race may be jeopardised by following a slower kart they've come up to lap. You're not forced to let them through, but it is common karting etiquette to choose a spot that won't lose you much time and allow them to pass you. Bear in mind, not all circuits/meetings operate blue flags (although letting the leaders through is still good practice – no-one wants to be the cause of ruining someone else's race).

Black

Displayed with the competitor's number, this requires a driver to stop in the pits within one lap and report to the Clerk of the Course. A penalty will ensue, which can include exclusion from the race.

Black/white diagonal

This is a warning flag, suggesting that your on-track behaviour is suspect and you may be black flagged upon further reports.

Black/orange circle

Displayed with the competitor's number, this indicates an apparent mechanical issue with the kart. The driver should proceed into the pits on the following lap.

Black/white chequered

This signifies the end of a race, qualifying or practice. Once you pass this, the racing ceases. You should slow down and proceed into single file back into the pits (or follow marshals' instructions).

RIGHT Official karting events entail some paperwork for all involved – such as the morning sign-on procedure for karters, and scrutineering cards (pictured) *(Enver Meyer)*

Race day procedure

While a little variation may exist, most events typically follow a set sequence that will soon become second nature. The following procedure is based on an MSA-licensed meeting. You may find that at other events, elements such as scrutineering and weigh-in are not necessary, and while you won't have your own kart to get race prepared as you'll be using one of the club's own machines, it is worth performing a quick check on your assigned kart for any loose bolts, deflated tyres, damaged chassis and other such issues.

Note that it is highly advisable for novice drivers to have got some practice miles under their belt before entering their first race.

Sign-on

BELOW At MSA events, equipment is checked by a scrutineer before anyone is allowed on the track. *(Enver Meyer)*

Having previously completed the club's race entry form and sent your payment, you should then have received confirmation of this, along with details of the day's schedule. In addition, new drivers will need to find out their race number and have the appropriate plates made up, ready for use on the day.

After arriving at the circuit with your kart fully prepared to race, you should unload it, get your equipment organised and then try to sign-on as soon as possible to avoid the potential rush later on. The club's staff will check your licence and club membership card. If you're racing as part of a team, all team members will obviously have to sign-on as well. Sign-on is usually around 8am so you'll want to be at the track at least half an hour before, if only to ensure you get a good parking bay (a rare commodity at some circuits), as well as some time to get yourself together.

Pre-race scrutineering

You should have been given a scutineering card at sign-on. This will need filling out with information such as chassis and engine numbers and handed over to the scrutineer. Scrutineering is the point at which your equipment gets checked for safety compliance. An official will verify that you're wearing the regulation race suit, gloves, boots, helmet, and inspect their condition as well as that of your kart. Again, it pays to get there as early as possible to prevent having to spend valuable time queuing up waiting for your turn.

LEFT Equipment that has passed scrutineering is often marked with an official sticker. *(Enver Meyer)*

Weigh-in

Take your kart, along with all the equipment you will be wearing for the race (ideally you will already have this on) to the weighbridge to make sure you'll be running above the allowed minimum weight. Remember to include your helmet, gloves and any other items such as rib protector and neck brace, and take the amount of fuel in the tank into account.

Each class of karting requires a specific minimum driver and kart combined weight to ensure a level playing field (a lighter kart will brake easier, accelerate out of corners quicker and potentially handle better, resulting in an unfair advantage). Drivers use lead ballast when required as any kart coming into the pits underweight is severely penalised.

BELOW When weighing in, remember to wear the exact equipment you will have out on the track, in order to work out the correct ballast. *(Enver Meyer)*

ABOVE Good preparation minimises the number of final checks required before going on to the circuit. *(Enver Meyer)*

Final check

Now is a good time to ensure everything on the kart is ready for action. Check bolts are properly tightened, that you've got the right tyre pressures, the fuel level, and lubricate your chain(s). Finally, make sure you know the day's race programme and which heats you are in, together with your starting positions for each. If you are racing in an endurance event, this is obviously a lot more straightforward, with practice immediately followed by qualifying and then a single race.

Driver's briefing

The driver's briefing is compulsory. It won't take you through every rule of the series you're racing in (you're expected to know those before you start racing) but it is an opportunity for the organisers to bring any issues relating to the day's racing to the attention of the competitors and to clarify any queries that may arise from these. Often, they will remind racers of the penalties for infringements, such as entering the pit lane with your engine running or ignoring any pit exit lights. There will be slight variations according to each circuit so it pays to listen carefully.

RIGHT The driver's briefing is compulsory and essential in finding out details of any particular procedures the club follows. *(Enver Meyer)*

Practice/qualifying

Practice sessions are usually cruelly short so get out as soon as you're allowed on the track. Use practice wisely, checking everything is in place and functioning correctly – trying to beat the lap record at this point is not advisable. In meetings with open practice sessions, you should then go back out and focus on your set-up and make adjustments accordingly. By the time qualifying starts (again, not applicable to all classes), you'll need to be happy with your kart and be focusing on putting in a good lap.

The race

Race start procedure alters depending on the class of racing but is limited to either standing or rolling starts. Green and red lights will usually be used for the start sequence but at certain tracks a national flag may be employed. This is raised to signify the start of the race on rolling grids, and dropped for standing starts. The race ends when the chequered flag is shown (unless stopped beforehand with the display of a red flag).

Post-race scrutineering

After the heats or final, karts will be called in by the scrutineers for checking to ensure they comply with all necessary technical regulations.

This is the same in endurance racing, when at the end of the event all karts are assembled after first passing through the weighbridge and are then checked by officials.

Trophy presentation

Assuming everything is in order, the top three drivers on the podium will be the same three that finished the race in that order. It's courteous to attend your

LEFT Know the flags, but also make a note of where marshals are stationed at the track. *(Enver Meyer)*

competitor's trophy presentation regardless of where you ended up and it further contributes to the sense of community so noticeable in many karting series.

Associated services

In addition to the essential elements mentioned earlier in the chapter, there are a multitude of further services associated with the sport. A handful of the more relevant examples are included below.

LEFT Winning your first race, or even making it on to the podium for the first time, can be an incredible feeling. *(Enver Meyer)*

RIGHT Lid designs that
are simpler and bolder
in approach tend to
work best.
(Enver Meyer)

BELOW Equipment
theft does occur, so
ensure you have the
appropriate insurance
cover. *(Enver Meyer)*

Kart schools

There are now a number of kart driving schools that offer varying levels of professional racing tuition, ranging from complete novices to experienced racers looking for that extra tenth of a second per lap. The quality of instruction can alter significantly between establishments so careful selection is advisable (particularly given the considerable costs involved), but for anyone wishing to speed up their learning curve or further hone their driving skill, a decent school can prove invaluable.

Chiropractic support

The lack of suspension coupled with forces experienced in karting inevitably compress your back, particularly if you're racing endurance series with lengthy stints. Several drivers regularly book a session with a chiropractor after a race weekend and swear by the benefits of this routine.

Lid design

By no means essential when starting out but as you progress you may want to consider a custom painted helmet. Several companies specialising in lid painting exist and most will also offer assistance with the actual design, should you need it. Remember that an overly intricate design may look impressive close up but a mess from a distance. Simple colour schemes not only look attractive from the spectators' viewpoint, but are also easier to spot. (While not directly related, it is a consideration that also applies to a kart's livery and can offer a certain strategic advantage.) A professional lid design isn't cheap, but if you get serious about karting it is desirable – it represents your identity on the track as well as establishing your status amongst fellow competitors.

Insurance

For those with life insurances, it is worth remembering that your policy may need to be amended if you start karting regularly. Your insurance provider should be able to discuss this and advise you accordingly.

As for specific karting insurance, there are specialised services offering storage and transit cover, personal injury insurance and, in some instances, even chassis on-track damage. Whichever cover you opt for, a basic storage and transit policy should be taken out. Karting equipment is expensive and thefts are, regrettably, an undeniable occurrence. As a further precaution, you should always keep a record of chassis and engine numbers in order to make stolen property more easily identifiable should the worst happen.

Costs

You'll often hear karting being referred to as a cheap form of motorsport. That's actually a contradiction in terms – there is no such thing as 'cheap motorsport'. But in relative terms, the above statement is true, although obviously costs vary wildly within the sport. The annual budgets for teams running at the high end of national, continental and world series, for instance, will easily exceed those of teams running in several other 'higher' categories of motorsport.

Having said that, you can have just as much fun racing locally on a comparatively minute budget. In addition, many of the series offered have regulations in place with the specific aim of controlling costs while also combating 'chequebook racing', the notion that the teams with the most money and therefore best equipment will be the ones consistently taking the silverware home. Furthermore, the emergence of 'arrive-and-drive' championships in recent years has also provided a hassle-free and cost-effective way of racing good spec, identical equipment within a friendly but very competitive environment.

Regardless of the category of karting you opt for, the reality is that it will cost you money. In addition to purchasing the equipment, owning your own kart means you will have to remember to budget for the running costs (eg consumables such as fuel, oil, tyres, bearings, spares, and so on), engine rebuilds, club membership, testing and race entry fees, insurance, travel costs, and accommodation (if applicable), for example.

It all depends on the level at which you plan to race, of course. The crucial thing to remember is that the more you spend isn't directly proportional to the amount of fun you will have – or guarantee an increase in performance. Many drivers will throw ridiculous sums of money at the sport, believing it will make them faster when that doesn't necessarily hold true. Making the right choices on equipment purchases (such as buying second-hand when appropriate) and its use at the track, being realistic about your driving level, and focusing on improving your technique before your kit, is a far more effective approach, and one that can keep your costs considerably lower.

BELOW Competing at higher levels can soon see costs increase at a frightening rate. *(Enver Meyer)*

3

The racing line

Photo: Enver Meyer

Introduction

While anyone can easily drive fast in a straight line, knowing how to maximise your speed through the corners is one of the fundamental principles of racing. Despite what some will tell you, it's hardly witchcraft and the basics behind this are quickly learnt. Mastering them, as with anything, will take a little longer.

When you think about it, the fastest line around a corner makes perfect sense. It's the trajectory that most 'straightens' the corner. In other words, the line offering the widest radius.

Consider how quickly you can drive through a wide open bend – a turn with a wide radius – compared with how much you need to slow down for a tight hairpin corner – a turn with a narrow radius. It stands to logic that as long as you widen the radius of any corner as far as it is possible to do so while staying within the boundaries of the track, you'll be travelling on the fastest line through it.

With that in mind, it then becomes important to understand the various components of a turn.

Turn-in

This is the point after the initial braking zone at which you should begin turning the steering wheel in order to get around the corner. Different corners require different rates of steering input but, generally, the position at which you start turning, combined with the degree of steering determines your next two points: the apex and the exit.

Apex

Also called the clipping point, the apex is sometimes described as the middle point of a corner. This is correct when referring to a constant radius line but as mentioned below, this would be misleading when dealing with a racing line. It is better to think of it as the point that separates the turn-in and the exit phases. This is usually the area that sees you closest to the inside edge of the track, which you clip before the racing line guides you to the outside of the circuit as you begin to reapply the power.

Exit

The exit point is where your kart should be at the end of negotiating the corner. In order to maximise the radius of a turn, the exit point is likely to require you to use all the track available, and sometimes a little more. It's not unusual to run right over the kerbs at the exit of a turn in the pursuit of the fastest line through it (provided the kerb design or run-off area allows this).

The right line

Having established the fastest line through a corner is the line with the constant widest radius, it's now time to work out the racing line. The two are not the same. This is because on a track you're not dealing with just a single turn but a collection of them,

ABOVE Your turn-in point is crucial because it determines the next components of a turn. *(Enver Meyer)*

LEFT Often, the apex can be found on the inside of the kerb itself. *(Darren Bourne)*

LEFT Remember that the fastest line through a corner is not necessarily the same as the racing line. *(Enver Meyer)*

The dotted line shows the constant radius through the corner, while the racing line is shown as solid – notice the later and sharper turn-in, later apex and therefore faster exit line

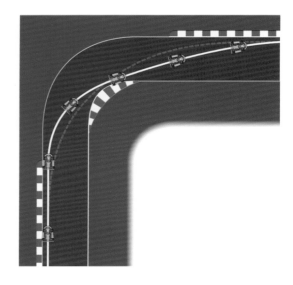

Taking the apex too early will usually make it impossible to get round the corner before running out of track, unless you slow down to correct your line.

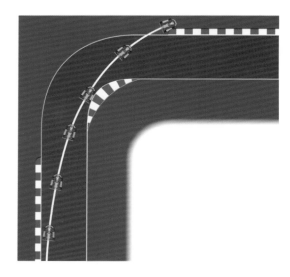

Apexing too late results from not being able to hit your turn-in point, usually as a result of failing to slow down enough as you approach the corner.

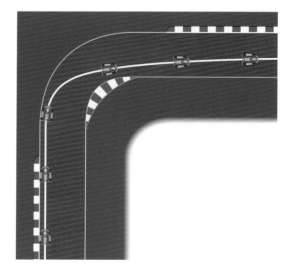

linked by straights. The straights constitute the majority of the circuit's length and are also its fastest sections, so, ideally, you want to spend as little time on them as is possible, meaning you need to travel through them as quickly as you can.

You achieve this by delaying your turn-in point so that you maximise the amount of time you're on the throttle before having to come off it to brake. In turn, this delays your apex so that it is now further around the bend than it would be on the constant radius line, and by doing so you actually end up with a straighter line out of the corner. This means you can start accelerating earlier so that by the time you reach your exit point you will be heading into the next straight at a faster speed.

At first, the racing line may not feel natural but with practice you will instinctively start to adapt your trajectory to ensure you go in and come out of corners in a manner that will give you the quickest way around a track. Bear in mind, also, that different karts may require slightly different lines through the same corner depending on their characteristics. Again, it all comes down to experience and plenty of practice.

One of the ways to get a feel for the racing line is to follow an experienced karter. Be aware though that some drivers get very precious about their lines and may deliberately feed you a 'dummy' line when they catch someone following them. Having said that, this isn't a common occurrence in many of the classes. Another option is to take the time to watch the good drivers as they're on the track and making a mental note of their braking, turn-in, apex and exit points. You are almost likely to always learn something that will help when it's your turn to get out there.

Getting it wrong

There are several ways to get the line into a corner wrong but normally most errors come down to apexing too early or too late. Hitting the apex early is usually the result of either turning in too early or too abruptly and unless you make some drastic corrections (involving a severe reduction in speed, sharper steering and, consequently, a very slow exit) you're likely to end up running out of track. You simply won't be able to get the right angle of turn to make it round the track (without slowing down).

Conversely, getting to the apex too late is normally an indication that you have taken too much speed into the corner, weren't able to brake in time and were forced to turn-in too late and too sharply. The result won't be as dramatic as the example above and your exit line will look invitingly straight, but unfortunately you'll be lacking the speed to put it to any use.

Types of corner

It is unlikely that you will ever find the same corner on every track you visit, of course, and while you have to take each turn on its individual merit there are however general approaches that can applied to cover most of the corners you will face.

Single apex

The majority of single apex corners are relatively straightforward and differ mainly in the angle of the turn. Assuming they are preceded and succeeded by a straight, the racing line shouldn't be affected. Aim for a late turn-in, being careful not to overdo it, then clip the inside kerb a little later than the constant radius line would have you do, and you're back on the power, heading towards the very outside edge of the exit.

Hairpin

Although technically a single apex corner, hairpins typically require an even later turn-in, meaning the initial steering input will be sharper which is acceptable due to the lower speeds involved. You'll be aiming for a very late apex and, as a result, the best way to build your speed back up as quickly as possible as you exit these slow corners.

Double apex

In the majority of cases, the way to treat these corners is to think of them as a single apex turn. As a result, the apex will not be by a kerb near the inside of the turn but rather at a point on the track

ABOVE Getting the right line is the result of much practice and a methodical approach to learning the track. *(Enver Meyer)*

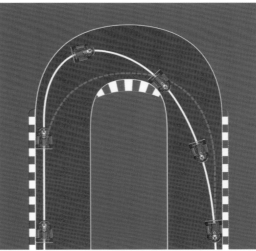

LEFT Hairpins almost always require a sharp, very late turn-in, so as to hit a late apex and maximise the exit speed.

LEFT Arguably the trickiest aspect of a hairpin is working out the braking point. *(Enver Meyer)*

Most double-apex bends actually have a single apex at a mid-track point between the two obvious apexes. (The racing line is exaggerated in this illustration due to width restrictions.)

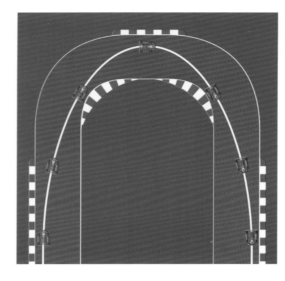

The two examples of variable radius corners are shown below.

itself. For instance, on a symmetrical double apex bend this would be between the two corners, probably mid-way on the actual track itself. Depending on the nature of the double apex turn, this can be one occasion when the constant radius line is actually the most desirable line.

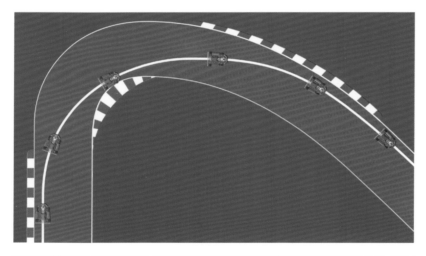

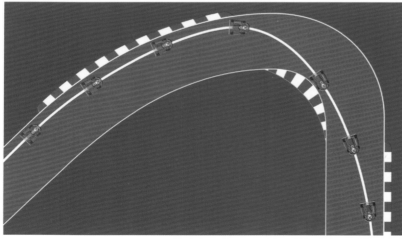

Variable radius

Variable radius corners refer to turns that either open up or close in as you go through them. In the case of the latter, you'll need to resist the temptation to steer towards the centre of the track as it starts to bend and instead, stick to the outside for a late and sharp turn-in. This should give you the opportunity to get back early on the throttle as you clip the apex and exit the corner using a wide, speed-friendly radius. In cases when the corner starts tight before opening up, take a slightly earlier and gentler turn-in, aiming to apex a touch earlier than if this were a 90-degree turn, and make use of the fact the track unwinds in front of you to maximise throttle application.

Chicanes

Chicanes cause a lot of people a lot of trouble but they don't really deserve their reputation. If you think of them as separate corners joined without the usual straight you would find between them, it's actually a lot easier to work out the ideal line. But it is important to realise that unless you're dealing with a very open chicane which you can almost straight-line (ie drive through with little or no variation in either throttle or steering application), you're likely to have to compromise one corner for the benefit of maximising your speed through the other.

The first thing to establish is whether the two corners are identical in radius. If they're not, then you should usually focus on getting your speed through the one with the widest radius. So, for example, if the first corner is displaying the tightest angle you should alter your turn-in to apex much later in order to keep your exit line towards the inside of the turn (which becomes the outside of the next turn, of course) which will then give you the best approach to tackle the second corner in a way as to ensure the fastest exit speed possible. If the situation is reversed, you'll be coming into the chicane on a straighter, faster line which will force you to the outside of the first corner exit phase, meaning you'll be too tight and therefore slow going though the second turn. This is acceptable, however, because the time saved as a result of the extra speed taken through the first turn more than compensates the time you lose by compromising your line through the second.

If the two corners are identical then it becomes a matter of comparing the straights immediately before and after the chicane and establishing on which of the two, will maintaining speed benefit your lap time the most. At times, this can be as simple as picking the one out of the two that is longest, but the track design will often also come into play – with experience, analysing this becomes easier. If it

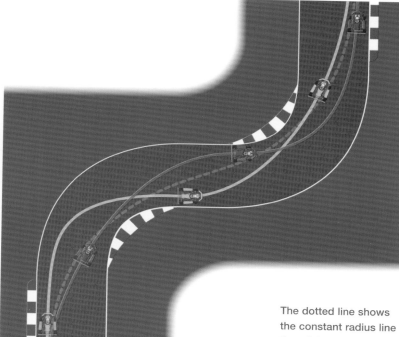

is at the initial straight then you'll have to sacrifice the line into the second corner by taking the line that maximises your entry speed into the first. If, however, the second is more important, then the corner line to compromise is the first, as you'll want to exit the chicane carrying the most amount of speed you can manage.

Learning the track

It shouldn't surprise to you to learn that until you know a track, you're unlikely to go round it very quickly. Learning the intricacies of a circuit takes time and while some are relatively easy to master,

The dotted line shows the constant radius line though both corners of the chicane, while the red line shows a trajectory that compromises the chicane exit in favour of a faster entry (conversely, the yellow line shows the opposite).

ABOVE Track walks are essential, particularly if you're new to a circuit. *(Enver Meyer)*

it's unrealistic to expect to have nailed all of the appropriate lines after your first outing. Then again, unless you manage to secure decent testing or practice times in advance, many of the race meetings you may enter as you start karting are likely to occur at a track whose characteristics will be completely unfamiliar. So you'll need to learn as much of it, as fast as you can.

Famously, triple F1 champion Ayrton Senna was able to easily spend two hours happily describing every detail of the track surface of a particular circuit. For most people, this isn't a level of affinity they may ever reach, but all drivers should be able to develop the ability to quickly accumulate a great deal of knowledge from a track, and eventually get to know it intimately, provided they follow a systematic approach.

Track walk

Walking the track, certainly if you're unfamiliar with it, is an essential part of learning the best way to go around it. Nothing beats sitting in the kart, going

RIGHT Elevation changes on a track are likely to have either a positive or negative effect on your kart's handling. *(Enver Meyer)*

around corners and working out the right line, of course, but you can guarantee that the track will look and feel very different to when you're walking around it.

That's partly because by speeding around a circuit, you inevitably miss a lot of the detail that you're able to pick up from touring it at a far more leisurely pace. Also, seeing it from the higher perspective of a standing position gives a certain advantage in this regard.

You should be noting changes in elevation and camber, and paying particular attention to track surface irregularities such as bumps or different patches of tarmac, and how these may have to affect your line (or change their characteristic when wet, for instance). It may be better to drive around them.

This is also the perfect time to be assessing kerbs, working out which can be safely ridden without causing possible damage to your kart, and those you should stay away from, as well as noticing any potential safe run-off areas should you find you need them during a race.

ABOVE LEFT Pay particular attention to surface changes that could affect performance. *(Enver Meyer)*

ABOVE Before riding kerbs, determine whether the profile of the kerbing is likely to damage the kart. *(Greg Richardson)*

LEFT The 'dirty' side of the track isn't a misnomer – stray off the racing line and you're likely to struggle for grip. *(Chris Walker)*

Finally, you may also want to pick out reference
points for braking, turn-in and exit points, although
this is arguably better suited from the perspective
of being sat in the kart. Nevertheless, it can be a
useful way of confirming the decisions you'll
subsequently make.

One thing to remember is the fact that to
maximise the usefulness of a track walk, you
should follow the racing line on your way round
the circuit. This ensures you're assessing the
right sections of track – in other words, the ones
you will be driving over – rather than areas that
you're unlikely to ever set a wheel on.

Finding the limit

When going out on to a track for the first time,
many beginners make the mistake of driving
around simply learning its orientation. If you're at a
race meeting, this isn't going to be of much use
when you come up against some competition.

You should be using any practice time you have
to find the limits of the circuit, and to find them,
you're going to have to go past them. If you watch
experienced drivers at a new track, you'll often see
them going off the track with surprising regularity.
This, in a sense, is quite deliberate.

Take braking points (braking is discussed in the

next chapter). How will you know how late to brake without first finding out how late is too late? The ideal way of working this out is to brake consistently later into a corner, lap after lap, until you can no longer get the kart to slow down enough to make it round to the apex (this may mean you run wide or even off the circuit). If you're being systematic in extending your braking point, the spot at which you applied the brakes on the previous lap will be the braking point for that corner. (Note, you should also try this slightly off line and find the absolute latest braking point to still be able slow the kart down and control the line to the apex for when it comes to putting an overtaking move on a competitor – see Chapter 6.)

Similarly, your entry speed into a turn should be increased systematically with each lap, until you run wide of the apex or at the exit. Again, the correct entry speed will be that applied on the lap immediately prior to overdoing it.

Obviously, with set-up changes you can further refine your line around a track but when you need to learn it quickly you should consider devoting any practice time you have to learning your way around, even at the cost of any set-up time. This is because, as a beginner, you'll save more time per lap by working out how late to brake and how much speed you can take around corners with a neutral baseline set-up (which should be how you approach any new circuit and from which you can subsequently tune your kart to suit the track's characteristics), than by having a correctly set up kart but not knowing the correct way around the track in order to properly exploit your vehicle's handling.

Reference points

Once you've worked out your brake, turn-in, apex, and exit points, you'll want to make sure you hit these every time you go around. Rather than trying to remember these instinctively, you'll need to pick reference points on the track, based on which you'll know when to brake, turn-in or where to aim when exiting. Unless there is a permanent irregularity such as the start of a new section of tarmac, for instance, it is not ideal to pick a reference point on the track surface itself. Generally, marks such as rubber or oil or even chassis scuffs will rub off over time, and sometimes even during the same race.

It's better to look trackside for your visual references, but again avoid things such as stones, grass patches or anything that can alter by someone driving over it. Concentrate instead on the noticeable feature of a kerb (such as damage) or on the trackside boundary. In the interest of accuracy, try to keep your reference points as close to the track as you can get them.

4

Kart control

Introduction

Once you know the correct way around a track, you then have to focus on maximising your driving skills. Your ultimate goal as a driver is to control a kart at the limit of its and your ability, for lap after lap. Being quick over one lap in every five isn't of much use when you're racing. You want to be consistent to the point of only varying your lap times by just a tenth of a second or two.

Not much room for error, then, but error isn't something top drivers are in the habit of committing.

Consistency comes from smoothness and a calm approach, but also an understanding of the dynamics at work on your kart and how these affect its handling characteristics.

Understanding tyres

Tyres are the single most important element of a kart. They are, after all, what connects you to the track. Everything that happens, everything you feel, everything a kart does, goes through the black rubber rings you find at the four corners of the chassis. Chapter 9 touches on the core aspects of tyre dynamics but for the purpose of kart control, it's important to understand some of the fundamentals at this stage.

Traction

A crude way of describing traction is to think of it as the amount of grip generated by a tyre. This is affected by a combination based on the type of tyre compound used (the hardness of the rubber, with the softer options providing more grip), the amount of load (or force) acting down on the tyre, and the coefficient of friction of the track surface and the tyre (the level of abrasion between the two elements; in other words, how easy the two slide along each other).

In karting, as with most forms of motorsport, the quickest way around the track requires you to be on the absolute limit of traction. Once you exceed it, the tyres lose their ability to grip and you pay the price in the form of a skid.

If you understand that the level of traction is limited and that a tyre can accelerate to the maximum of its traction threshold, brake using all of its traction or steer relying on all of its traction, you'll understand why it cannot do all three at that level at once. But it could theoretically do all three provided you balance the demands on the tyre so that, when combined, the three do not require more than the total level of traction available.

In reality, karting only requires tyres to handle two of those things simultaneously – you're either on the brakes and steering, or you're steering and on the accelerator. At every other time you'll be solely either on the brake or the throttle, and judging the traction available in those situations soon becomes second nature.

Learning to balance the simultaneous demands on a tyre and knowing how to push to the very limit of traction is obviously crucial for fast cornering and, by extension, a quick lap.

Slip angle

A tyre's slip angle refers to the difference between the direction a tyre is pointing and the actual trajectory it is travelling on. At slow speeds, the tyre will follow exactly where it's pointing, meaning the slip angle is zero. However, as speed increases, so does the slip angle. Too much slip angle means the kart is drifting wide and losing speed and is therefore undesirable. But so is too little slip angle – if you're not sliding slightly through corners, then there's more speed available and you should be going faster. The ideal slip angle, the point at which tyres generate their maximum ability to grip, takes a while to assess correctly and is mostly a case of trial and error until you develop a feel for it.

Load

This is another way to describe the amount of force, or weight, being placed on a tyre. When accelerating, most of the load will be on the rear wheels as the weight distribution transfers to the back – just think about how you're propelled back into your seat when you bury the throttle. Conversely, when you brake the majority of the load moves to the front wheels, along with the weight transfer (again, think about needing to push against the steering wheel when braking

hard in order to stay in your seat). And, of course, when going around a corner, the weight distribution shifts to the outside and it is therefore the outside wheels that take on the most load.

Contact patch

Having understood load, it is easy to grasp the concept of a tyre's contact patch, also known as footprint. As either of its names suggest, this is the area at the bottom of the tyre that is in contact with the track, and it is what gives a kart its traction. The size of the contact patch depends on the size of the tyres and the amount of load that's placed on them. If you think that load on a tyre effectively works in the same way as placing a large weight on top of it, then it is easy to imagine how the contact patch would increase in this case as a result of the tyre being squashed down on to the track. From there, it is only a short step to accepting the fact that a larger contact patch will give you more grip, in other words, more traction. Reducing the load, therefore, reduces the contact patch, which in turn decreases the level of traction. This directly affects a kart's handling and will manifest itself in corners as either understeer or oversteer, the explanations of which you will find later in the next section of this chapter.

Basic kart dynamics

The caster effect

All karts have a single rear axle that doesn't feature a differential, a component used in cars that enables the two rear wheels to rotate at different speeds. In a straight line this isn't an issue but think about what happens when you go around a corner. The outside wheel has to travel

Understeer results from a lack of grip at the front tyres in relation to the rear.

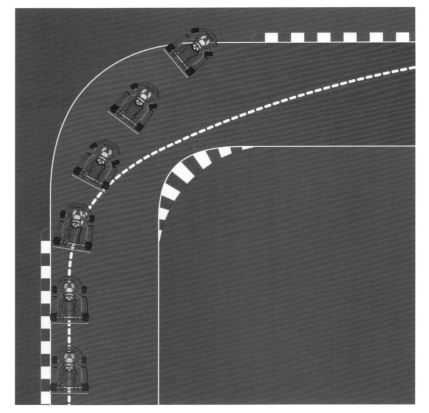

along a wider radius – and therefore spin more – than the inside wheel, and it can't do that when the rear axle doesn't allow the two wheels to rotate at different rates to each other. So every time you turn in a kart, you're effectively scrubbing the two rear tyres against the track – the inside wheel is being forced to rotate further than it needs to while the outside wheel's spin rate is being restricted by that of its counterpart at the other end of the axle. This obviously affects your overall speed.

The way a kart alleviates this is by relying on the caster effect to help it. Caster is the change in the angle of the spindle, the part of the steering assembly that attaches to the wheels. When you apply the steering in a kart, caster drives the inside wheel downwards and the outside upwards, meaning the outside front of the chassis drops. As a consequence, this helps lift the inside rear of the chassis and therefore the rear wheel, meaning the outside rear wheel can carry on its wider trajectory without being impeded by the inside wheel, and the kart therefore turns.

Understeer

This is caused by front tyres having less grip than the rears, meaning that, as you're turning, the kart will push straight on and refuse to go in the direction the front wheels are pointing towards. In slow corners this is obviously very costly by making it exceptionally difficult to get the kart to go around the bend. On fast open bends, a small amount of understeer can actually be useful and make it easy to predict the kart's trajectory.

Oversteer

Surprise, surprise, oversteer occurs when the front wheels have a higher level of grip than the rears. The kart will therefore change direction quite happily but, suffering from a lack of traction, the back-end will step out of line and you end up with a tighter turn radius than anticipated. Obviously this has its advantages in certain tight corners but in medium-speed turns it can often result in a spin if the driver fails to correct the back-end slide in time.

Driver input

A common mistake made by beginner kart racers, from watching other drivers, is that they assume because of the dart-like nature of karts when you see them on the circuit racing against each other, that kart control inputs should be lightning quick and the driver should be working frenetically at the wheel. In fact, it is completely the opposite. You want to be as smooth as you possibly can with the controls because that's the fastest way to get round a track.

Steering

If you've read the above section on how a solid rear axle affects cornering you're probably thinking

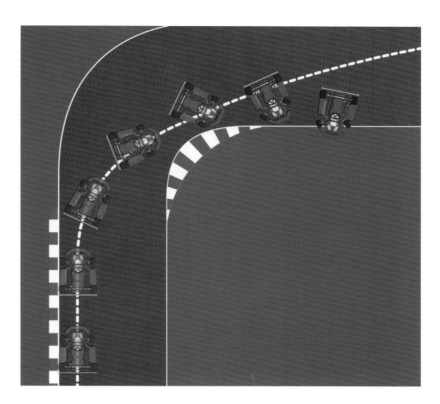

you're best off not turning the wheel at all. Obviously that's not going to help with getting around a track but now that you understand how much effort the engine has to make every time the

When the front tyres have more grip than the rears, a kart can oversteer – the back-end will tend to slide out of control.

LEFT Ideally, kart control inputs should be smooth and minimal. *(Enver Meyer)*

ABOVE LEFT When steering, the outside hand should be doing most of the work. *(Enver Meyer)*

ABOVE RIGHT Gripping too tight on the steering wheel increases the risk of mistakes. *(Enver Meyer)*

BELOW There should be a slight overlap as you roll off the brake pedal and start applying the throttle. *(Enver Meyer)*

steering wheel is turned, you'll appreciate why it's crucial to keep steering input to the absolute minimum. In a perfect world, you should aim to nail the racing line without having to make a single directional correction on your way around the lap.

This requires absolute precision in your steering, and is best achieved by being as smooth as you possibly can. Experience will help in getting a feel for the kart and instinctively knowing how much steering input is needed but this is helped immeasurably by looking well ahead (as discussed below).

It is also important to know how to turn the wheel. It sounds silly but it actually makes a difference to how a kart handles. On a left-hand turn, the majority of the force when turning the wheel should come from the right hand pushing

upwards. Logically, then, on a right turn, it's the left hand doing most of the work. By pushing on the steering wheel, you're also adding more load on to the outside front wheel which, as you should know by now, will help you make it around the corner.

Lastly, keep your grip relaxed. Holding on to the steering wheel as though your life is dependent on it will prevent you from being smooth, you won't be able to interpret all of the handling feedback the wheel offers, and will quickly bring on muscle fatigue. This is particularly relevant during endurance events – relaxing your hands during long straights will help reduce any discomfort, and which in itself can be an indication that you're holding on too tight.

Pedal input

By now, it shouldn't surprise you to learn that the way you apply the throttle, come off it, apply the brake, lift off and get back on the gas should be done as one continuous, smooth motion. You should always be on one pedal or the other and, fractionally, on both as you make the transition between them. Be particularly careful not to rest your foot on the brake pedal as you're driving and 'ride' the brakes to the point of needing a new clutch or a new engine from overstressing and heat build up – unless you're applying the brake, your left foot should be off the pedal. Developing a fluid style to pedal application ensures any weight changes the kart undergoes are not abrupt to the point of severely disrupting its handling, making its behaviour more predictable and, ultimately, you quicker.

Rolling off a pedal and squeezing another doesn't mean it has to be as slow and weak a movement as it sounds. Actually, the very nature of racing requires your braking to be contained in the shortest area possible, meaning you have to be

LEFT A straight back, shoulders parallel with the back of the seat, head high and both arms and legs slightly bent – the ideal kart posture. *(Enver Meyer)*

quick and hard on the pedal, but that doesn't mean you can't do so with great sensitivity. In fact, it is vital because you'll want to be able to feel for things like the rear wheels locking up and immediately easing off the pressure, if so required.

Equally, when you feed in the power you'll want to achieve full throttle as early as you possibly can, but you need to do this progressively. On more powerful karts, too much throttle too soon will usually see the rear wheels break traction, possibly resulting in a spin. Sensitivity will develop with experience, of course.

Posture

Good posture in karting is essential. There are instances when you will need to alter your pose in terms of helping your kart's handling, and these are discussed later in this chapter, but for the most part your back should be straight, your shoulders parallel with the back of the seat and your head held high.

Your head should also be straight – many beginners (and indeed drivers who should know better) have a tendency to dip their head as they turn into a corner, which is understandable because it feels natural. But it will not allow you to have the best vision as you're going round the track and will hinder your performance. If you watch the top drivers, they will almost always keep their head firmly straight and their body rigid so as to minimise any potential effect on handling (other than when it may be necessary to shift the weight balance, again as detailed below).

LEFT Hunching forward while driving is rarely advisable, unless you're trying to reduce drag when on a long straight. *(Enver Meyer)*

Vision

Movement follows your vision. It's one of the reasons why so many drivers get stuck into the rhythm of the kart in front of them – because that is where they are focusing their attention and their actions instinctively adapt to get them to where they are looking.

But once you know this, you can obviously use it to your advantage. The goal is to get to a stage that allows your subconscious to take over the majority of driving duties so that, effectively, you are driving on autopilot (this is helped by visualisation, discussed in Chapter 7). This will enable you to focus on where you want to be, which is obviously ahead of where you are currently, and for your body to react almost automatically in order to perform the actions necessary to get you there.

In other words, when you are approaching the corner and you're hitting the braking and turn-in points, you will want to be focused on the apex. By the time you reach the apex, you should be looking at your exit point. Once at the exit, your focus should now be on the next braking or turn-in point (depending on the track ahead), and so on.

In practice, this isn't at all easy to achieve because it essentially forces you to 'switch off' and ignore your conscious mind's insistence on controlling the here and now, and as such requires

ABOVE AND BELOW
Experienced drivers tend to keep their heads straight at all times.
(Enver Meyer, above; Greg Richardson, below)

This has the additional advantage of being interpreted as a dominant and potent stance by onlookers. Top drivers aren't simply fast; they look fast, too, and they're more than happy to share this with the competition hoping it may intimidate some of them when they meet on the track.

a level of confidence and experience most beginners will not yet have. Moreover, for most drivers it will feel utterly unnatural, but it is important to practice and persevere with developing your subconscious skills because it is likely to have a considerable effect on your driving and lead you to lap times you would not expect to be able to achieve. You will instinctively make adjustments to steering, throttle and brake input with a delicacy that you would find difficult to match when trying to do them consciously. Your lines will be more accurate and display the type of consistency associated with the top drivers. So the sooner you learn to do it, the better.

Advanced techniques

Trail-braking

Technically, trail-braking is an advanced control method, but it is crucial to learn how to do it as soon as possible. Some karting schools prefer to wait until a driver has mastered the art of braking in time for a corner before they then introduce it, and there is certainly some logic in that, but provided you fully understand the requirements involved, it is probably wise to get to grips with it from the moment you start karting.

Trail-braking is a way of maximising your entry speed into a corner, while minimising the amount of time lost through braking on the preceding straight. So your braking point is actually further along the straight than a conventional braking point. This requires braking very hard for a short concentrated

ABOVE You should always be looking ahead of your current track position. *(Greg Richardson)*

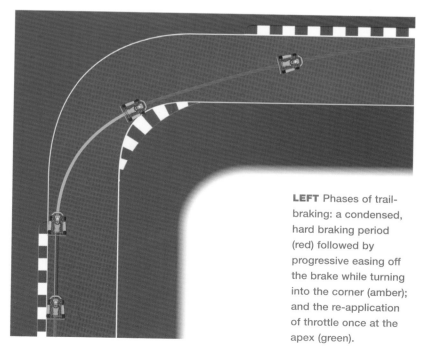

LEFT Phases of trail-braking: a condensed, hard braking period (red) followed by progressive easing off the brake while turning into the corner (amber); and the re-application of throttle once at the apex (green).

period on the straight (known as threshold braking), using all of your tyres' traction ability.

Then, as you initiate the turn-in, ease off the brake pedal. Note this is not the same as coming off the brake fully – you will need to stay on it, continuing to scrub off speed and progressively easing off the pedal as you get closer to your apex. At this stage, you're balancing the steering against the braking, taking care not to exceed your kart's level of traction at any point.

Usually, just before the apex, once the kart has rotated into the correct position (an added benefit of trail-braking is the fact it loads the outside front wheel, therefore helping lift the inside rear wheel and getting the kart to turn quicker), your steering lock should be unwinding, you'll be nearly completely off the brake pedal and the time has come to start feeding the power. This will briefly overlap the brake input as you roll off one pedal

and on to the other (on clutch karts, it's a good idea to start your acceleration a little earlier still in order to ensure the clutch is disengaged as soon as you need the power to exit the turn). By the time you hit the apex, you should be off the brake and on the throttle, which you then increase progressively as you make your way out of the corner.

A further advanced technique, and useful for some corners, is to deliberately exceed the traction level of the rear tyres during the turn-in phase and let the backend step out in order to get the kart to rotate towards the apex more quickly than waiting for the front wheels to do their job. This in turn should allow you to get on the throttle earlier but be careful not to overdo it or risk spinning off.

Body weight shifting
One of the reasons karting is so physically demanding is that you should be using more than

BELOW Oversteer can prove useful for certain corners, enabling you to set up the kart for the exit earlier than would be the case without sliding the back-end.
(Greg Richardson)

LEFT Upper body movement within the seat has a significant effect on handling, and is a crucial part of the driving technique, particularly in wet or damp conditions. *(Enver Meyer)*

just your arms and feet to get around the track quickly. With karts being relatively light, your body is the heaviest single unit of the entire driver/kart set-up. As such, you can have the most effect on handling by altering the overall weight distribution, and you do this by simply moving your upper body in the seat.

Even a relatively subtle amount of movement will have a noticeable effect so don't start contorting yourself beyond recognition. You want to be able to help the handling while still being in a position to control the kart at the limit, and you won't be able to do so if your helmet is scraping along the track with you bent over the sidepod.

The idea, then, is to lean to the outside of a corner in order to transfer more weight on to the outside rear tyre. By further loading this tyre, you help increase the level of traction, while simultaneously assisting in the unloading of the inside rear tyre which, as already discussed, has to lift in order to enable the kart to get around a turn.

Shifting your body weight is particularly useful in wet conditions when a lack of grip becomes a significant issue, and should be done with delicacy, particularly when applied during a high-speed corner. Tighter turns will benefit from a more determined and accentuated movement (usually also towards the front so as to load the outside front tyre), but in both cases it is crucial to practice your leaning so that you learn how to execute this technique without negatively affecting your chassis's handling.

Easier ways of using your body weight include leaning slightly back on the rear axle to increase the load transfer on to the rear wheels which helps gain extra traction during threshold braking into corners, and also when accelerating out of the exit phase.

Elbow lock

If you consider that the entire kart chassis is designed to flex around you in order to get itself around the track, then there's obviously ways that you can accentuate handling characteristics by the forces you apply on the frame from the comfort of your racing seat. The effects of pushing on the steering wheel have already been mentioned, but an additional technique involves locking the outside steering arm at the elbow while cornering. This effectively uses your body as a conduit to transfer load from the front end on to the outside rear wheel. In practice, this is a way of helping counteract a kart with oversteer tendencies while you're out on the track. It is not as effective as performing the appropriate set-up changes, of course, but it can certainly help when you have no other option of dealing with it. (By contrast, flexing your arm will help combat understeer.)

Mid-corner braking

Some of the top drivers can settle a kart through a high-speed corner by applying a little brake while still accelerating, ensuring that vital engine rpm is not lost. How successful and desirable this technique is will depend on the class of kart you race – it's a good way to burn a clutch, for instance, so you may want to focus on finding the right setting instead.

(Chris Walker)

Wet-weather racing

Introduction

Many drivers fear or genuinely dislike racing on a wet track, but that's actually the wrong attitude to take. It is little coincidence that Ayrton Senna and Michael Schumacher, two of the most talented racing drivers the world has seen, were both rain masters, able to leave the rest of the field standing when track conditions got slippery.

Racing in the wet, apart from being a necessity if you want to be a complete driver, will actually improve your overall standard. It forces you to be ultra smooth and helps you get a better appreciation and feel for where the traction limit is. It is also a great equaliser because advantages such as power and chassis nuances are both minimised. By contrast, driver error is amplified.

Being prepared for wet weather racing will also make a huge difference to your performance on the day. It is vital to be suitably protected against the rain because if you get cold and wet, you may find your concentration is affected, your muscles will certainly contract and you'll lose sensitivity and smoothness. In addition, your reactions slow down and fast reflexes are crucial for wet weather racing because the kart can handle in a completely unpredictable manner and as such, you need to stay sharp.

So invest in a decent wetsuit but because these are not guaranteed to keep all of the water out, take a change of socks, T-shirt and underwear with you so that you can put those on and don't get cold between heats or stints. Ideally, you'll also want to have a spare pair of gloves and boots that you can use while the other ones are drying. Consider an anti-fog treatment for your visor and maintain a tiny gap when shutting it to allow air to circulate, further reducing the possibility of the inside of the visor misting up. Finally, drill two holes into the bottom of your kart seat. They won't affect its structural integrity but will allow any collected water to drain, meaning you don't have to drive around the track as though you're sitting in a paddling pool (and carrying more weight).

Still, as much as it may be uncomfortable to get wet and is tedious to have to thoroughly dry and clean up your equipment after the session, you should actively look for wet days to practice. You should even consider going out on slicks – apart from forcing you to concentrate on your inputs even further, it could come in useful the day it starts to drizzle mid-race and coming in for wet tyres isn't possible. However you get out there, just make sure you clock up some mileage in the wet because, ultimately, it's experience that will make you a faster driver in the dry. If you approach a rainy track with that attitude, you will always come away feeling a lot better about yourself and your performance.

OPPOSITE Racing in the wet can do wonders for your overall driving skills and, despite the obvious discomfort, drivers should welcome wet conditions. *(Greg Richardson)*

LEFT Preparation for wet weather racing extends beyond the right overalls and tyres – you'll need to have the right mental approach, too. *(Enver Meyer)*

Technique

There is only one way to drive in the wet, and that is to be smooth, smooth and then smooth. Both brake and throttle need to be deployed with extreme sensitivity. If you're too aggressive on the anchors, the wheels will lock up and you're likely to spin off the track – you certainly won't be slowing down.

If you're too quick on the accelerator you'll get wheelspin and go nowhere fast, or may even find yourself facing the wrong way.

Even with grooved rain tyres, a kart will understeer severely in wet weather. The first time you turn the wheel in such conditions (and you'll generally want to turn in earlier then you're used to), you're likely to wonder if the wheels are still connected because the kart will simply carry on in a straight line, to the point where you think you're going off the track. Don't panic. A kart will stubbornly ignore directional commands until speed is low enough for the front tyres to bite, at which point it turns sharply. You just have to trust the fact that the grip will come, but it takes a while before this situation stops being unnerving. It is crucial that the kart is under power while doing this – it simply will not coast around a corner in the wet – and this is also the reason why trail-braking isn't the best approach for a quick wet lap.

On some karts, a trick is to snap the steering wheel to full lock going into a corner in order to accentuate the caster effect and try to get the inside back wheel to lift, and just as quickly start to unwind the lock as soon as the kart shows any sign of turning (not doing so will probably see you spin out). You can still do this smoothly though.

Even if the above technique isn't suitable for your kart, a driver's posture during wet weather driving is more universal. As you steer into a corner, lean your body towards the outside front

RIGHT The smoothest drivers tend to benefit the most in the wet, as steering, brake and accelerator inputs get amplified. *(Enver Meyer)*

wheel, again to try to help unload the rear wheel so as to encourage the kart to turn by loading the outside front tyre. How much you lean and how violently you do this depends on how tight the corner is – generally, the tighter the turn, the more movement is needed. As you exit the corner, sit back into the seat in order to get some weight back on the rear axle for grip. Feed power through gently until you're back on full throttle.

Driving in the wet will initially feel messy and very slow. The thing to remember is that almost everyone else will be thinking the same. It is actually possible to get into a very satisfying flow, gently balancing the throttle out of corners and linking one bend with the next, while always remaining highly alert for any signs the kart is about to do something unexpected. It takes experience and the only way to obtain it is to get out on a wet track whenever possible.

RIGHT By comparing a
standard wet line (blue)
to a standard dry line
(dotted), you can see
the two only meet to
cross over each other –
in the wet, there is
usually more grip on
the sections of the
track that see little
action during dry races.

The wet line

Generally, the easiest way to explain the wet line is
to say that it runs completely off the dry line. This is
because the dry racing line will typically have a
deposit of rubber from constant use (as well as
fraction deposits of chain lube, fuel and oil) and this
becomes treacherously slippery as soon as you
add water into the mix. So on a wet track the grip
tends to be on the sections of tarmac that you
would never want to drive on during a dry race but
that become desirable in these conditions because
often rain water has a chance to soak into the track
(rather than lying on top of the racing line and
becoming the jam in what is effectively a rubber
sandwich if you were to drive over it).

In a corner, driving on these sections usually
means driving on the outside of the racing line (note
this isn't necessarily the same as driving around the
outside of the corner). But every track is different
and this isn't always the case. For instance, in high
speed turns the line is likely to be identical to the dry
equivalent, albeit with a fair amount of understeer
that you wouldn't obviously get without the rain.

At come circuits, even a slow corner may have a
wet line that is very similar to the dry line.
Unfortunately, finding the wet line is mostly a
process of trial and error, further compounded by

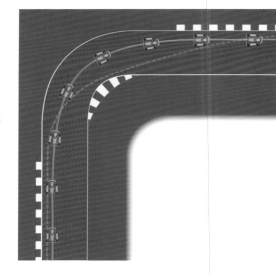

the fact that a circuit's characteristics can change
remarkably quickly depending on the amount of
water on the track.

The best advice is to have confidence in your
own feel for the kart and not to be afraid to
experiment with different lines, however odd they
may seem, in order to find the fastest way around
a wet track. Again, take some comfort from the fact
that a lot of the time the majority of the other
drivers won't necessarily be too sure about what
they're doing, either.

BELOW The wet
racing line will usually
be off the dry line.
(Enver Meyer)

Drying track

If you thought driving on a wet track was difficult, think again. Few occasions in karting will demand as high level of concentration as dealing with a drying track. Expect to alter your racing line on lap-by-lap basis in order to keep finding grip. As a result, the lines you use may seem even more extravagant than the full wet line you might have employed a few laps earlier and will require you to mix elements of dry and wet weather racing.

The trick when trying to determine the grip levels of new lines is to not stray too far from your previous lap's trajectory. Try to keep a systematic approach to your driving. Doing so keeps you from any potential nasty surprises that could see you careering off the circuit.

Remember that a track can dry quickly when the weather has suddenly changed for the better, combined with the amount of other drivers going around dispersing the standing water. This creates an additional problem with regards to your wet tyres which are made of a soft compound (in order to maximise their heat and traction capability under cold wet conditions) and that they will therefore rapidly disintegrate when used on a dry surface. Obviously, with a drying

track it is only a matter of time before you need to change to slicks, but while the advantage is still with staying out on wets, then you need to do your best to keep them cool. Running over wet patches during the straights, for instance, will help prevent them from overheating before you're due a new set of slicks. (And when you do change tyres, remember to also alter your wet weather settings back to a set-up more favourable to dry conditions.)

ABOVE Success in the wet only comes from much practice. (*Enver Meyer*)

BELOW A partially wet track can be treacherous. (*Enver Meyer*)

Set-up

Chapter 9 gives an overview of how the main set-up changes affect a kart's handling, albeit with a primary focus on dry track situations. Therefore, and in the same way that you should keep all equipment relating to wet weather driving in one container, so as to make any potential changes in between races (or, indeed, mid-race) to a wet set-up more efficient, it seems appropriate to include general settings advice relating to a wet track within this chapter.

As with any settings change, it is important to test their effect one at time. Remember, too, that it is possible to go too far and make the kart more difficult to handle. Lastly, bear in mind that most wet settings are undesirable for dry track racing. If the weather is expected to improve throughout the race (more applicable for endurance events), then a compromised wet set-up is a better solution than subsequently losing too much time in a pit stop changing everything back to dry settings.

Centre of gravity

Because of the general lack of grip on a wet circuit, getting the chassis to flex becomes more difficult. This is one of the reasons why chronic understeer sets in, because the kart is effectively lying too 'flat' on the track as it is going round. One way of counteracting this is to raise the centre of gravity, which puts more force on the chassis to flex. You can achieve this by raising or even just tilting the seat forward. Relocating any lead weight to the top of the seat will also help.

Back-end settings

As unloading the inner rear tyre becomes more difficult in a wet track situation, you'll want to reduce the rear track width. This decreases the radius difference between the two rear wheels while cornering and helps combat understeer.

Also, stiffen the rear bumper. Further stiffening the chassis with the addition of a torsion bar (if the chassis allows it) will also assist in lifting the inside rear wheel in turns because of the way it is affected by wet weather front-end settings, but remember that this can come at the cost of traction, and especially so if you happen to be racing on a particularly bumpy circuit, for instance.

Front-end settings

Contrary to the rear, the front-end track should normally be widened and the front bumper

loosened. This will help increase grip for better turn-in, as well as contributing to getting the inside rear wheel to unload.

In addition, lowering the front ride height can also be useful in adding more front corner load, helping the kart in turns.

You will want to increase toe-out (the wetter it is, the higher the setting – 15mm is not uncommon) to improve turn-in capability. Also, this will keep the front tyres scrubbing as you're going round, which helps

keep their temperature higher and therefore provide better grip. The low temperature and low friction level of a wet track prevents the tyres from overheating.

Generally, it is also a good idea to maximise the caster setting and increase positive camber. Try out different settings to get a feel for their effect, and bear in mind different designs will offer a variety of opportunities. Only by testing extensively will you build up the necessary knowledge of your kart's characteristics.

BELOW Decent turn-in ability on a slippery track comes from increasing toe-out, caster and positive camber settings. *(Enver Meyer)*

Racecraft

Introduction

It is one thing to be a great driver but quite another to be a great racer and even drivers of exceptional natural talent have to develop their racing skills. Good racecraft combined with driving ability guarantees success but takes years of experience to acquire. Thankfully, the highly competitive nature of the sport means there's no better way of learning this than through karting.

Overtaking

Top drivers make overtaking look effortless but appearances can be deceptive. Getting past the competition is one of the most satisfying aspects of racing but it takes years to master, and it is crucial to know the concept of the racing line intimately, which is why overtaking is only dealt with so late in the book.

There are, in effect, two main methods of getting past the opposition. The easiest is to out-drag them on a straight, having taken more speed from a good exit out of a corner and using a competitor's slipstream to get an additional advantage in order to get past them more easily. Or, you can out-brake a competitor on the approach to a corner – the tighter the corner and the longer the straight leading to it, the better your chances. Other ways exist, of course, but they are less common and can often rely on irregular situations or a competitor making an error.

LEFT A good example of out-braking a competitor into a corner and gaining a position. *(Enver Meyer)*

Planning

A good driver will usually plan most overtaking manoeuvres in advance. For example, it may be necessary to follow another kart for a couple of laps to assess any areas of weakness that could be exploited. Even then, the deciding move is likely to have been initiated from a previous corner, giving the driver the additional speed they will need to be in a position to attack. Indeed, in karts where keeping momentum is key it is often necessary to hang back a little to get a run up on your competitor – timing this takes both experience and precision planning.

Stay alert

While planning overtaking manoeuvres is important, it is equally vital to be prepared to pounce on any unexpected opportunity to make up a place. For instance, when in a convoy and the kart in front makes a move on a competitor, it is quite typical for the driver being passed to be caught off guard and be thrown off his line just long enough for you to also make a move. Alternatively, the two may tangle, handing you two places in one go. Learning to fully exploit situations such as these soon becomes an integral part of winning drivers.

Pressure

While you would never want to get past another driver by throwing them off the track – there's little merit or reward from that kind of tactic – there is nothing wrong with forcing them into an error of their own doing by keeping them under pressure. A very gentle nudge at the odd corner will remind them that you're still behind and possibly get them thinking about you rather than focusing solely on the road ahead, which in turn may lead them to miss their braking point and presenting you with an opportunity, for instance.

Slipstreaming

Anyone who watches motorsport will know about the slipstream effect – the notion that a car closely following another suffers less drag due to the vehicle in front doing all of the work of cutting through the air, and as such it enjoys a power advantage over its competitor which it can use to overtake. The principle applies in exactly the same way to karting and on long straights getting behind another kart offers a definite speed gain (some drivers even tuck their heads in towards the steering wheel to further reduce resistance) that could make the difference needed to complete a passing move before the next bend. Timing the move is important but so is being smooth. Many drivers dart out violently from the back of the kart they're following at the very last moment, and then lose the speed they've gained from their unnecessarily brutal movement.

ABOVE Pull smoothly out of a competitor's slipstream at the last minute. *(Enver Meyer)*

LEFT Notice how close the overtaking kart has remained to number 20. *(Enver Meyer)*

LEFT If you've been overtaken, don't dwell on it – it happens. Instead, focus on sticking to your competitor's rear bumper. *(Enver Meyer)*

RIGHT Out-braking a competitor into a corner is one of the more common passing moves. Remember that you only really need to position your kart alongside at the turn-in point to effectively claim the corner and, subsequently, the position.

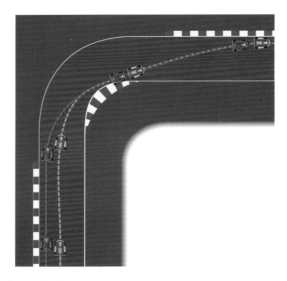

Getting it right

Successfully out-braking a competitor into a corner requires you to get alongside them during the braking zone in a way as to ensure they are aware of your presence so they don't turn in on you. Obviously, it's crucial to know just how late you can leave your braking, which is why it's important to practice this outside of the race itself (as discussed in Chapter 3).

How far you need to be alongside before you can claim the corner is likely to remain a matter of discussion for eternity, but generally, if you've managed to get your front bumper past the halfway point of the your competitor's kart you're in a strong position. You'll have the inside line and they are forced to either attempt to go around the outside, which is unlikely to succeed, or yield and tuck in behind you.

When instigating the move, you will want to stay as close to the racing line as possible, as this will give you as fast a line as you can hope for in the circumstances. An added advantage of this is that should your competitor turn in on you, they are unlikely to be carrying enough momentum to affect your trajectory or send you off the track. When overtaking, many beginners do so too far away from the other kart, compromising their own line into the corner and making it easier for a competitor to re-take their position.

Getting it wrong

It is not unusual for a passing kart to get it wrong when trying to out-brake a competitor. They will often over-estimate their braking, normally because

ABOVE In this shot, number 27 is a fraction too far back – but also too far away – to claim the corner and position. *(Enver Meyer)*

RIGHT An example of an overtaking manoeuvre executed correctly. *(Enver Meyer)*

they've come from too far back to have a genuine chance of making the move stick. The extra distance they will need to cover, compared with a correctly judged pass, usually means having to stay on the throttle and off the brakes for longer, and many drivers just leave it too late and run too deep into the corner, thereby handing you an opportunity to retake your position. It would be rude not to.

Defensive line

Driving a defensive line successfully will stop the kart behind you from overtaking by discouraging them from attempting a move on you. But it comes at a price and that is a slower lap time. Generally, you're having to move away from the racing line in order to cover the inside of a corner where a competitor is likely to attempt an out-braking manoeuvre. This effectively means having to negotiate the corner on a tighter radius, which requires you to go slower into and through it. The good news is that you maintain control of the line and the kart behind you doesn't have much choice other than to follow. The bad news is that if you're not in the lead, the competitors ahead of you will be getting away.

It is important to realise that driving a defensive line has its time and place. In the closing stages of a race, you'll obviously want to keep any threatening competitors behind you. However, at an earlier point in the event it may be wiser not to fight too hard for the position, stick with the driver once they've passed you and attempt a move on them

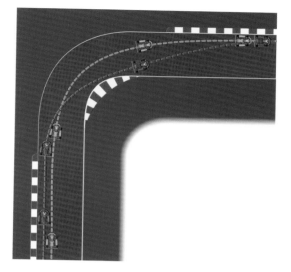

LEFT Leave your braking too late while trying to pass another driver and you will gain a place, which is soon retaken by your competitor as you invariably miss your turn-in point and the apex, leaving you with a slow exit.

yourself at a later stage. It is not uncommon to see races where two drivers work together to catch up with the leader rather than waste time trying to block and pass each other. This is one of the reasons why you'll sometimes see a kart pushing another on a straight – the speed advantage this offers is a strategy to either catch another rival or to distance themselves from the chasing pack. Once they're clear or up with the leader, then the racing resumes. As with a lot of aspects of karting, using your head can make a real difference to your success. It is also worth noting that often a far better tactic than defensive driving is to focus on a cleaner, faster lap. If your competitors can't catch you, you won't have to defend.

BELOW Driving defensively is a skill that forces opponents to take lines that rarely prove successful for overtaking. *(Enver Meyer)*

RIGHT Right and wrong techniques for defending your position.

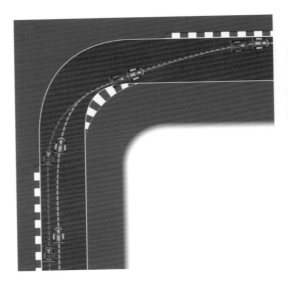
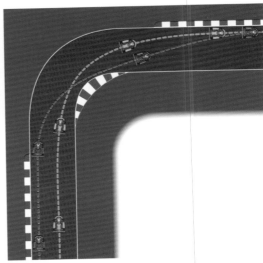

Furthermore, be realistic about your level of driving. As a beginner, you're unlikely to be able to hold your own against experienced drivers. Making it unnecessarily difficult for them to pass when they are theoretically much faster than you is ultimately pointless and won't make you many friends. The same still applies if you are experienced but are suffering due to a kart with a performance-sapping mechanical problem.

Perhaps most importantly, remember that driving defensively is not the same as blocking which involves weaving on the track, is usually illegal, and likely to quickly result in an accident (or you being punted off the track by an infuriated competitor).

Getting it right

A defensive line won't obviously work on a straight whereby a competitor with more speed will simply drive around you. So its use is primarily for approaches to corners where you're under threat from having another driver diving in on the inside and taking your place. Ideally, then, you'll want to position your kart to follow a more central line, forcing the following kart to think twice about going for the inside line and attempting a move on the outside instead. The latter is unlikely to be successful because going into the corner you should still be marginally ahead and you can then control the line and the pace out of it.

Getting it wrong again

A typical mistake is to move too close to the inside edge of the track when defending. Again, this invites the driver who's trying to pass you to go round the outside. However, due to narrower angle of entry you have created for yourself, you're either going to have to slow down excessively or take a deep exist in order to get around the corner. This may be enough for the other kart to slip in front by simply taking the normal racing line or, if you do still manage to get to the inside kerb first, to drive around you on the virtue of carrying considerably more speed.

Being overtaken

The trick to dealing with being overtaken by a competitor (and it will happen, particularly in as closely fought sport as karting, so you should learn to not let it affect you psychologically), is to lose as little time and momentum as possible while it happens. Normally, if a faster kart is behind you they will find a way past and as long as you're aware of your surroundings, you should carry on driving your normal line. The responsibility is on the overtaking kart to perform the move safely and effectively.

If there are a number of competitors following in close formation then it becomes crucial not to lose

BELOW The smartest drivers lose the shortest amount of time when conceding a position. *(Enver Meyer)*

too many positions as a result of the first kart overtaking you. When the kart behind has made a move, give it enough room to get by but stay close – this should indicate to the other drivers behind that you are in no mood to leave the gap open and will close this as soon as the first kart has got through. It should discourage them from attempting a move themselves and it will stop you from being 'left hanging out to dry' with no option of getting back on the racing line until they've all waltzed through. However, this is not a guarantee that a second kart won't follow through so keep an eye out when attempting to move back into position.

Dealing with traffic

Almost always, one of the differentiating qualities of champion drivers is their ability to slice through backmarkers and only losing a negligible amount of time in the process. For mere mortals, making your way through traffic can be a convoluted and very costly affair but there are ways to minimise the effect on your lap times.

Be noticed

By their very nature, backmarkers may be inexperienced and as such are likely to be completely oblivious of the fact that you're right

behind them. A friendly tap on their rear bumper will alert them to your presence and is likely to see most of them soon waving you through.

Be careful

If the blue flags are out, don't simply assume the kart you're trying to lap has seen them, or that it is going to respect them. If you're attempting a pass up the inside into a corner, make sure you can do so safely should the kart in front decide to turn in, still on the racing line.

ABOVE & BELOW Top drivers cut through traffic without losing significant time – a crucial skill.
(Both Enver Meyer)

RIGHT Unless you get
used to dealing with
traffic on the track,
you're unlikely to
get to the top step of
the podium with
any regularity.
(Enver Meyer)

Be decisive

As with any overtaking manoeuvre, it's easy for
beginners to feel apprehensive about making a
move because they're likely to be envisaging every
scenario that could go wrong. As a result, any
attempt at overtaking is tentative and indecisive
which in turn greatly increases the likelihood of an
incident. If you're going to make a move, assuming
you're confident you can make it stick, then you
have to commit to it the same way you commit
yourself to corners. However, it is something you
build up to, so don't expect to be at ease with it
from the very start.

Be tactical

For karts where building up momentum is an issue,
such as prokarts, it's imperative to try to time where
you're going to catch up with a slower backmarker
in order to get past them with the minimum loss of
speed. This could mean you have to hold back a
little, rather than driving right up to their bumper in a
part of the circuit unsuitable for overtaking, getting
stuck and then not having the necessary speed
advantage to make a move when the right occasion
presents itself.

Be opportunistic

If you're behind another leader who you're racing for
position and you both come up behind a
backmarker, don't think twice about capitalising on
the fact they may be slowed down and are
vulnerable to being overtaken.

Equally crucial is not being left behind if your
competitor does put a move on the backmarker. Try
to sneak through at the same time as you can't
afford to be caught up behind traffic while your
competitor pulls away into the distance. But be
extra careful the driver being passed doesn't close
the door without realising you're also attempting to
overtake. Try to minimise a chance of this
happening by getting right on the bumper of the
kart that's doing the overtaking.

Racing etiquette

Being lapped

Regardless of whether or not your club utilises a
blue flag system to indicate to drivers that a leader
is trying to overtake them, it is common courtesy to
let them through. (And in the case of impatient and
unnecessarily aggressive drivers, it may also stop
you from finding yourself shunted off the track.) That
doesn't mean you should immediately pull over to
one side, slam on the brakes and roll out the red
carpet, but as soon as it is safe to do so, and
ideally in a manner that won't lose you too much
time, point to the side you would like them to pass
on and give them room to do so.

One common mistake beginners often make is
to point too late, usually just as they're about to turn
into a corner. Or as they accelerate on to a straight,
somehow expecting the faster driver to have the
speed advantage to beat them in a drag race

situation. This is unlikely, unless the lapping driver has managed far better exit speed out of the bend.

Still, a preferable solution to having to lift off in a straight (as this will severely affect your momentum and therefore lap time) is to let leaders through on a slower part of the circuit, such as the entry to a tight corner. You can usually tuck in right behind them and learn something from their lines, and without losing a considerable amount of time.

Signals

Not so much etiquette as common sense, raising your hand when you spot a yellow flag alerts drivers behind you that something is wrong ahead and they should take caution. This signal is also used for when you're heading into the pits to let others know you're no longer racing and they should overtake you, and again, if you suffer a mechanical breakdown or there's something with your kart or yourself that prevents you from carrying on racing.

Accept responsibility

The importance of how other drivers perceive you is looked at in Chapter 7, but it is obvious arrogance isn't one of the attributes you'll want associated with your name. If you're the one at fault for a race incident then it is both courteous and important, after the race, to approach the victim you may have accidentally thrown off the track or aggrieved as a result of an error, to explain yourself and apologise. That should stop any ill feeling from carrying over to the next meeting and any potential retribution you

may have suffered by not clearing the matter up, putting you in unnecessary risk and possibly costing you dearly in terms of the championship you may be contending.

Marshals

It is always good practice to take the time to thank the marshals as you drive around the track on your in-lap. After all, they keep you safe, can help get you back on the track and you wouldn't be racing if they hadn't shown up.

ABOVE You should always race hard, of course, but also fair. *(Enver Meyer)*

BELOW Karts come without hazard lights, so use a hand. *(Darren Bourne)*

RIGHT Some accidents
are unavoidable, most
are not. *(Chris Walker)*

Accidents

No matter how safely you drive, and despite the
fact that karting is supposed to be a non-contact
sport, you're bound to be involved in an on-track
incident at some point during your racing. The
nature of motorsport makes this a highly likely
eventuality rather than a vague possibility. However,
it is worth keeping in mind that in karting the vast
majority of accidents tend to be minor off-track
excursions or on-track spins, which are either self-
caused or assisted, but rarely dangerous. Serious
accidents do occur, of course, which is why it's
imperative to race with your brain switched on and
to be paying attention to the action on-track at all
times during a race. There will be times when
contact is unavoidable, granted, but that doesn't
mean you shouldn't actively try to keep those
occasions to a minimum.

Avoidance

Like most accidents, racing accidents are usually
the result of stupidity. Alas, it is a regrettable reality
that innocent drivers will often also get caught up in
them and pay a costly price for someone else's
lack of judgement or moment of madness.

In karting, the majority of accidents can normally
be summarised to include someone going for a gap
that doesn't exist, attempting to squeeze out a
passing kart, refusing to accept they've been

overtaken and claiming a corner that is no longer
theirs, losing control under braking and taking the
kart in front with them, or a backmarker not being
aware of their surroundings and turning in on a
leader they hadn't realised was there. There are
others, of course, but these will cover most
situations. While avoiding them all is unrealistic, it is
possible to stay out of trouble on many occasions.

If you're doing the overtaking, judge it well and
go for a gap as long as you can get there safely,
without the other driver turning in on you because
you're too far back for them to see you. Last-minute
lunges are very exciting, but if it's an overambitious
move you're better off sticking where you are,
working to close the gap up and trying again at
another opportunity.

Don't fight lost causes. If a kart has pulled up
alongside and has the line into the corner, don't try
to squeeze them off the track. By all means stick
with them around the outside if you can but
recognise when the fight is over, accept it will
happen, and learn from it. You're better off
concentrating on maximising your speed through
the corner in case your opponent makes a mess of
things, enabling you to take your place back, or
tucking in neatly behind them and trying to re-pass
them later on, rather than both ending up off
the track.

Should karts in front of you collide or spin,
immediately scan the track for a gap. This is when
looking ahead particularly pays off, because it will

give you more time to react. If the karts have yet to stop moving, it's actually a good bet to aim for one of them because it's unlikely to still be in the same spot by the time you get there. If you point at a gap and the karts are still spinning it's possible you could be driving straight into their path. Also bear in mind that a kart whose driver has lost control will usually spin towards the outside of a corner so steering towards the inside could usually work out well for you. Whatever you do, don't maintain your gaze on a spinning kart. As mentioned earlier, there is a tendency for humans to go where they look so if you focus on an out-of-control kart you'll often find yourself headed straight for it, or even spinning off in sympathy.

Minimising the penalty

If you do spin off the circuit, don't sit there and gesticulate wildly either at yourself or the competitor that's caused the incident (and who may well still be racing on the track). Get out of the kart as soon as you can and it's safe to do so, turn it to face the right way and get yourself going (remember not to drop the kart onto the track after getting it to point the right direction but lower it back down gently instead so you don't damage it). By being stationary, you're losing vital seconds that are almost impossible to make back up on the track. Once you're moving again, clear the incident out of your mind. It has passed and there's nothing you can do to avoid it now. Focus on the race ahead and how your strategy may have to change in order to salvage something out of your new situation.

At times, it's easy to think after an incident that all hope is lost but that kind of mentality won't get you very far. It's perfectly possible to end up with a very respectable result following a spin or venture off the track. Remember that other competitors can suffer a similar fate, or even mechanical failure. The point is you can't know what lies ahead so you may as well give it all you've got until the chequered flag is out, and see what happens.

Effect

A big accident without serious injury can still have a significant effect on a driver. It's important not to develop an irrational fear as a result of what can be a genuinely traumatic experience. All accidents have a logical cause and taking the time to analyse the reason behind them should obviously teach you something about potentially avoiding a similar incident in the future but, importantly, it should also get you to overcome any apprehension you may have suffered as a result of it. The best drivers always learn from their mistakes but they don't dwell on them, either.

Regaining your composure after accidents also becomes gradually easier as you get better and achieve success regularly. Not only because you learn to avoid – or at least fully understand – a lot of the situations that caused early career crashes, but also because the hunger for winning overcomes the hampering effect accidents can have on a driver. Ultimately, you have to accept it as a risk of the sport and not let it hinder your future performance.

LEFT If your kart remains drivable after an off, immediately focus on getting it back on the track as quickly as possible. *(Enver Meyer)*

7

Physical and mental preparation

Introduction

A champion driver will be able to drive right on the very limit for every lap of a race without showing a drop in performance. They may have an exceptional level of talent, sure, but they are still human. What marks them apart from the also-rans will no doubt be their completeness as a driver: outstanding racecraft, a superior level of dedication, great physical condition, and a finely honed mental approach. Learning how some of these areas can help unlock your full potential as a racing driver is obviously crucial to success.

Fitness

Although the average onlooker will assume that drivers are simply sitting there pushing pedals, turning a wheel and letting the kart do all of the work, karting is a very physical activity. It should therefore come as no surprise to learn that if you're not physically prepared for the demands of the sport, you shouldn't expect to be winning.

The benefits of fitness and its effect on various aspects of an individual are well documented. Your performance, not just in terms of stamina but psychologically, too, is directly affected by your physical condition. A karter with a high degree of fitness won't get tired throughout race day, will retain higher levels of concentration, make fewer mistakes and maintain their competitive edge until the final chequered flag of the day comes out, resulting in higher levels of confidence.

Being fit enables a karter to better deal with the strain of g-forces experienced while racing, it helps alleviate mental fatigue, increases your reaction times, enhances your physical endurance and raises your heat tolerance. The last point may seem more appropriate to an F1 driver stuck inside a oven-like cockpit, under the blazing sun of some exotic overseas location while wearing several layers of fireproof materials, but temperature is the number one enemy of a driver, regardless of the discipline they race in. You may be open to the elements in a kart, but even on a mild, overcast day the physical exertion of driving a kart successfully while wearing your race gear will see most individuals get very hot and bothered. If you're not fit enough to deal with this, your performance will suffer substantially – just a two per cent drop in hydration has a noticeable impact on physical levels.

However, you will find that at clubman level only a minority of drivers take peak fitness seriously enough to invest the time and effort to improve their physical condition. This is therefore an opportunity to secure a sizeable advantage over your competition.

The ideal training will concentrate on upper body strength and stamina, the two areas most applicable to kart racing. Generally, driver fitness is made up of stamina, spirit, strength, suppleness and reaction speed. Any exercise programme should focus on working on these intricacies while also building core strength – it's not just bulk and muscle (in fact, too much will affect your kart control). The easiest way to ensure a well-rounded programme is to engage in other sports – swimming, cross country running, climbing, rowing, cycling, racquet sports, and gymnastics are just some examples of activities that actively contribute towards a driver's overall fitness make-up. And, of course, it makes training a lot more fun than spending hours down the gym.

It's important to be organised and also be taught to train properly. Fitness experts recommend training between three and five times a week, with a full day off from all activity – remember that over-training can be damaging (and dangerous). Aside from the health benefits, consider the additional advantage that regular exercise – in combination with a full, balanced diet – will have with regards to helping regulate body weight. Given that the easiest performance boost you can achieve in any form of motorsport is through weight reduction, ensuring you're not overweight will maximise your kart's power-to-weight ratio.

Ultimately, working out your own programme of fitness and sticking to it is essential for your improvement as a driver. Because the last thing you need is to be worrying about whether you're fit enough to compete at an event – it takes the attention away from what you should be focusing on. (Of course, you shouldn't undertake any form of exercise plan without first consulting your doctor.)

Stretching

The importance of stretching before any form of exercise is vital in preparing the body – both physiologically as well as psychologically – for the physical strain that lies ahead. Due to its high physical demands, karting is no different. Just because you're not at your local gym doesn't mean the principles suddenly stop applying. You should therefore build stretching exercises into your race routine as a way of ensuring you don't cause your body any harm (this is particularly important for those planning to do a long endurance stint). As an added bonus, it can also be integrated as another way of triggering a mental response that should see you increasingly focused on the racing as the main event approaches.

Diet

Your everyday diet should obviously be well balanced to maintain a healthy body, but there are ways of tailoring it to better suit a racing driver's needs, such as ensuring a build up of glycogen (which the muscles use during exercise). This is typically obtained from carbohydrate-rich foods in the days leading up to the event. A trained dietician can help with this, although there are also books with plenty of advice and guidance on this subject. Here we are simply looking at an overview of the type of food you will require during the actual race day.

The right food, the right drink

It is crucial to maintain both your energy and concentration levels and this requires the right intake of food as well as ensuring you maintain yourself properly hydrated throughout the day. The ideal food should provide the required levels of energy without dehydrating you and this includes bananas, breakfast cereal, energy bars, and sandwiches with honey or peanut butter type fillings – all things that can be taken easily to the circuit.

Ideally, you'll bring something more substantial and packed full of slow-release carbohydrates (baked beans, wholemeal pasta or bread, porridge) Relying on getting food from facilities at the circuit isn't the best of ideas – at least in the UK, where the type of nourishment normally available appears to have been selected for its fat or sweet content, two things you'll want to keep to a minimum if you're going to maximise your performance.

It is also important to keep to familiar food. Race day is not the time to be trying out new culinary delights. You need to stick to a diet that you know works well for you.

As for drinks, commercially available isotonic beverages offer good liquid absorption rates as well as provide some energy content in the form of carbohydrates and are a good alternative to water. But you can easily make your own isotonic drink:

- 1 litre of fruit juice (or 200ml cordial)
- 1 litre of water
- 1 gram (pinch) of salt

In a situation where quick hydration is needed, go for hypotonic drinks which are absorbed much faster by the body. Again, these can be bought or easily made at home and brought with you to the circuit:

- 250ml of pure fruit juice (or 100ml of cordial)
- 1 litre of water
- 1 gram (pinch) of salt

Time your food and drink intake

You should actually aim to start your hydration process some 24 to 36 hours before race day by drinking little and often, continuing this routine throughout the race meeting itself (carry a bottle with you and this will soon become second nature). Remember to alternate between water and isotonic liquids (just water will end up flushing your body's minerals away) and drink more frequently during hot days.

It is not advisable to eat too close to the race start. To digest food, your stomach needs an

Taking on too much liquid before a sprint race can also leave you feeling nauseous, although particular consideration should be taken for endurance racing. With stints that can easily last an hour and a half, even the sweatiest competitor is likely to find nature calling while they're still out on the track if they've had too much to drink before getting in the kart – a considerable distraction when you're supposed to be focusing on your racing line.

Routine

Aside from dealing with the necessary elements of the big day, such as sign-on, scrutineering and the driver's briefing, the importance of getting into a routine for race day shouldn't be underestimated. But what many beginners forget is that this actually starts the night before.

Be organised

The worst thing you can do is get to a track late, rush through sign-on, scrutineering and still be making tweaks to your kart as the practice session opens. By the time you get on the grid your state of mind will be in utter disarray and you're unlikely to be properly focused on the task ahead. What's more, you will probably be playing catch-up all day, meaning you will never recover from the hectic start.

A lack of organisation can play havoc with the events of race day and completely ruin your chances of success. It is crucial to have everything ready the day before so that the kart is prepped and all set to race (bar any minor last-minute adjustments such as tyre pressure) and all your gear is packed and just waiting to be placed in the car or van.

Plan your journey in advance so that you allow the correct time to get to the track and try to get there early enough so that everything can be done in a calm and collected manner.

Sleep

It is vital to get a good night's sleep. If it's your first race, or a championship decider, it is natural to be tense but try relaxation techniques to calm your nerves. It is important to aim to get between eight and ten hours of decent sleep. Given the early start of most race meetings this may typically mean a very early night if you're having to travel there. Depending on how far you are from the circuit, you may want to consider finding local accommodation in a bed & breakfast or even sleeping at the circuit if this is possible and you have the appropriate facilities.

Wake up early

It is important to allow yourself to wake up gradually

ABOVE You should be as relaxed as possible before a race and able to concentrate solely on the task ahead. *(Enver Meyer)*

increased supply of blood to digest food, which is also what your muscles require when they're being used for physical activity – such as keeping a kart under control. Devouring your meal just before you step into the kart could result in severe indigestion. But even before that happens, you're likely to feel other effects sooner – being thrown around a track with a stomach full of food isn't particularly pleasant. Consuming a good carbohydrate-based meal two to three hours prior to hitting the track will give enough time to have digested the food and you can then follow this throughout the day with snack-sized additions (remember to really chew your food in order to break it down properly – otherwise your body will have to take large amounts of energy to do that itself).

to enable your brain to have the time to go through the correct procedure to reach its fully awakened state. Jumping out of the bed at the first sound of the alarm is not what you should be aiming for and it will affect your ability to perform behind the wheel throughout the day. Build time into your schedule to lie in bed for some 20 minutes or so, before getting up and getting on with your day. Don't rush, and do things methodically.

Track walk

A track walk, as discussed in Chapter 3, is an essential part of working out your racing lines but even if you know the track well, it should remain an important part of your race day routine. As you cover the track on foot, you can more easily visualise your performance and focus on the task at hand. Everything that happens before the race should be in place to get you into a mental state ready for what lies ahead. This is just one part of the package.

Relax

Whether they admit it or not, all drivers get nervous before a race to varying degrees; it's natural. Because everyone is different, there is no set pattern to follow – only you will know what works best from trial and error. Yet, if all else fails, there is a simple but effective last-minute trick you can do while waiting on the dummy grid, which is to clench your fists and your whole upper body as tightly as you can and then relax. Repeat this for a few minutes and you should feel the tension in your

body reducing with each cycle. By the time the race is ready to start, you should be in a relaxed but in a ready state of mind.

Focus

Some of the finest racing drivers often talk about a state of mind they reach, a point at which they feel totally at one with the kart and the track, and

ABOVE Try not to allow yourself to be affected by the commotion of the starting grid.
(Darren Bourne)

LEFT Being able to focus – and being able to get to that state quickly and consistently – is fundamental.
(Enver Meyer)

everything else ceases to exist. Ultimately, that is the level of driving you are striving to achieve.

It's another way of explaining that your entire being is solely focused on the task at hand. Focusing requires practice but is vital in allowing you to centre on the demands of racing without letting yourself be affected by the many distractions of the race environment.

Maintaining focus during the actual race is also something that comes with practice. For instance, don't think about a mistake of three corners ago.

Move on. Concentrate on the road ahead, not on what's gone behind. Similarly, don't get angry or be affected by the action of others. It's pointless and as soon as you get emotionally involved you lose control of the situation. Centre that energy on reaching a new level of driving and don't worry about what everyone else is up to.

Finally, don't be concerned about lap times or results. Your focus should always be on achieving the best performance you can, and the lap times and results will come as a consequence of this.

Driving aids

When it comes to improving your driving and racing skills, nothing beats track time. Obviously, factors such as time and money can limit access to a kart, meaning that while the desire to learn and improve is there, it may not always be possible to accommodate it in the best way possible. But there are alternatives, some of which you'll find below.

Visualisation

Visualisation or imagery is a technique favoured by sports psychologists and widely employed by competitors at all levels of sport. You'll often see racing drivers engaged in this before a race, usually when they are sitting in the car in the pits or on the grid. Visualisation requires you to imagine yourself driving on the track and to recreate every element of that situation so that your brain genuinely believes you are in the kart. It is entirely possible to reach a stage of visualisation that triggers emotional responses similar to those you experience while out on the track – you will 'hear' the engine and 'feel' the cornering forces, for instance – and to visualise a lap that is very close in time to the real-life equivalent.

This takes practice, of course. You won't be able to switch into this mode while you're waiting for your race to start amidst a typically hectic environment without the experience of knowing how to get your mind into the correct state. Regular practice at home, ideally by recreating the racing environment as closely as possible (so you should aim to be wearing your race equipment, holding a spare steering wheel and sitting in a spare seat – or better still, sit in the actual kart if this is easily achievable) is essential. In time, your technique will improve and your visualisation ability will become more powerful.

The benefit of visualisation is that, when done properly, it effectively creates a mental programme that your brain automatically reverts to once you're out on the track. In other words, you're letting your subconscious do the driving. Every braking and turn-in point, clipping the apex, maximising your exit speed, hitting the correct line on every corner, even starts can be practised through visualisation (while also eliminating bad habits) and it's experience that is directly transferable to when you're out on the track. Obviously, it stands to reason that you can have several 'programmes' (such as wet weather driving) that you can tap into when conditions on the racetrack change.

Note, however, that visualisation isn't the same as daydreaming. Imagining yourself winning the championship through a last-corner do-or-die overtaking manoeuvre won't exactly help with perfecting your driving ability. Imagery is an extremely useful technique that focuses solely on improving your skill as a driver but that requires a systematic approach and great dedication to perfection. The payback, however, can be priceless.

LEFT Good visualisation technique takes a lot of dedicated practice, but its effects are widely reported. *(Enver Meyer)*

Videogames

Arguably more fun than visualisation – although something you should consider as a supplement, not a replacement – is the use of videogames. It's not uncommon these days to hear of new touring car or even Formula One drivers using a videogame to help 'learn' a new track before a race weekend, such is the accuracy of their representation in the latest games.

Sadly, while other racing categories are graced by some excellent videogames, karting has so far suffered from poor virtual interpretations. But that's not to say opting for an F1 game, for instance, can't have its benefits. Crucially, you will want to use as convincing a set-up as possible, and this means investing in a good quality force-feedback steering wheel and, ideally, partnering it with a 'driving simulator' style seat. There are an increasing number of these available and while some offer an unsuitable driving position, there has been at least one model that not only featured a genuine kart seat, but that was designed by karters to provide a realistic driving position.

Still, however convincing the driving experience, it is obviously going to be a long way from actually being behind the wheel of a kart. But the benefit of employing videogames to help your mental preparation isn't in trying to duplicate track time in the sense of attempting to hone your kart control skills (although high-end simulators can certainly help in terms of getting you to drive smoother), rather to improve other important aspects. As such, racing in a virtual pack of cars (regardless of what category they may belong to) can help with spotting overtaking possibilities, for instance, as well as get you to think about correct track positioning.

If you alter the difficulty settings to deliver stern opposition, the best videogames will force you to work hard to catch, let alone stay ahead of, the competition. Combine this with real-life length races and maintaining the required levels of concentration for such long periods of time is great conditioning for when you get back in your kart, particularly for those who favour endurance racing.

But even on a virtual track free of competitors, today's videogames are so graphically detailed and the handling models so advanced that controlling a videogame race car can help you practice elements that you should apply on a real circuit, such as the picking of braking and turn-in points, trail-braking, the effects of camber, caster or toe-in changes, and even the crucial habit of looking through the corner, ahead of your current position.

There's no suggestion videogames are ever a substitute for real practice, of course, but they can be a valuable aid in terms of helping reinforce the racing mentality required for on-track success. Perhaps best of all, they're hardly a chore.

Radio-controlled models

Another genuinely useful, although equally fun activity is radio-control (r/c) model racing. Legendary F1 driver, Ayrton Senna, was passionate about his collection of r/c aeroplanes which he reportedly flew with remarkable flair. The eye-hand coordination necessary to expertly control r/c models is of great value to a racing driver as they are skills that are directly transferable to driving. In addition, it's an activity that also requires high levels of concentration, which again is a benefit that is applicable to race conditions.

Racing r/c cars, which you can do easily at local clubs all over the country, has the added bonus of relating even more directly to kart racing because the cars will need setting up correctly in order to perform competitively. Tyre choice, camber, toe, and a multitude of other adjustments can be made and their effect is certainly noticeable, helping reinforce the thinking behind the kind of set-up decisions you make at the track.

Mind games

If you have ever followed a whole racing season on television, you will have noticed drivers will often play mind tricks to try to gain an advantage over the competition. Often, this is done via the media, with specific comments during interviews made for the sole purpose of unsettling their opponents psychologically. Sometimes it works, sometimes it doesn't, not least because everyone is different and what might unsettle one person will have little or no effect on another.

Obviously, kart racing doesn't command anywhere near the same amount of column inches that higher profile motorsport categories enjoy but that's not to say the principle of gaining a psychological advantage over the competition isn't just as valid. Indeed, it is arguably even more crucial in karting because the chances are most drivers have yet to fully develop the appropriate defence mechanisms against this.

So the plan here is to provide you with some psychological artillery, so to speak, to get you better armed for dealing with the kind of mental ammunition fellow competitors are likely to fire at you. Because it's worth remembering that while karting can usually remain in the realm of friendly

LEFT Like any other form of motorsport, psychology plays a large part when it comes to achieving success in karting. (Enver Meyer)

competition at nearly every level, it is still competition. Competition inevitably brings out a side in people that isn't necessarily there in normal everyday conditions.

Don't believe the hype

Consider the driver who, having comfortably beaten a rival subsequently states during a friendly post-race chat that they were hampered by a mechanical problem, thereby suggesting their ultimate pace should have been faster still. There may indeed have been an issue with the kart, but it's equally possible this has been exaggerated or indeed fabricated entirely as a way of inflating their perceived driving ability. An impressionable driver may be affected by this kind of revelation to the point of thinking it fruitless to attempt to regain a position after being passed by said driver during a subsequent race, feeling that he ultimately lacks the necessary pace to match his opponent when in reality the two are more evenly matched than the perception of the 'slower' driver suggests.

As in other areas of life, drivers will attempt to establish a 'pecking order' on the track, and they do this in part by their actions off the track. So it's important to keep an objective outlook at what is said by drivers before and after races, on Twitter or posted on Facebook, knowing the only elements you can accurately assess are those extending to your kart and your ability. That is not to say you shouldn't respect your competitors, not least because at this level there is always bound to be someone who is

genuinely faster. But the crucial element is to try to remain unaffected by what you hear – and, specifically, what someone may want you to hear – and have confidence in your own skill while being realistic about your development as a driver.

Be realistic

Unlike the way a kart accelerates, for instance, developing your driving ability wouldn't be represented on a graph as a continuously progressive line. Instead, it would more likely plateau at several points, perhaps even dip, although the overall progression would be positive. Too many beginner drivers get despondent when, after quickly acquiring some skill, their rate of improvement appears to stagnate, or when they don't seem to be making progress in terms of catching the faster drivers, or feel unable to match the talent of the frontrunners.

The thing to keep in mind is the fact that the likelihood of going up against someone whose talent you may never match is possible. But that doesn't mean you can't beat them and you should give up – after all, even during Ferrari's dominant years, Michael Schumacher didn't ever turn up at a race to find out the rest of the F1 paddock had stayed at home because they felt there was no point in even trying. It's also worth keeping things in perspective with regards to your current level – ask yourself how, given the same experience and equipment, your chance of success might otherwise fare. That is by no means the same are resigning yourself to being beaten, or trying to justify a relative lack of pace or skill. It is simply a realistic, objective view of the situation. Having self-belief and confidence can obviously make a tremendous amount of difference to a driver's performance and indeed they are a vital part of their make-up, but it is equally important not to fall into the trap of overconfidence which can be as destructive as a lack of it.

As a beginner, you'll be battling with drivers with more experience and skill. Rather than letting it frustrate you, take comfort from the fact that, as with any sport, facing up to better opponents will inevitably speed up your rate of improvement. The only way to progress your development as a driver is to continually find challenging situations and going up against a similarly skilled rival will usually elevate the standard of both drivers on to a new level.

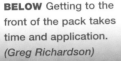

BELOW Getting to the front of the pack takes time and application. *(Greg Richardson)*

Remaining at your local kart track because you can beat all-comers is neither likely to provide long-term reward, nor significantly improve your skill.

So set yourself challenges, by all means, but be realistic about your expectations. To put this into perspective, even someone with three years' regular racing will still be considered a rookie by some karting schools. By achieving challenges that require genuine effort and applied concentration, but are not impossible given your current standard, your confidence, and by extension, your performance will improve.

Take a break

Many of the techniques you need to learn to be a successful kart driver take many years to master. At first, you will probably struggle with the amount of

new information you're having to digest and it is easy to find occasions when you're trying something new and you're simply not improving, and possibly getting worse. Take a break, switch your engine and your mind off for a while. When you get back in the kart things will usually have fallen into place, your new skills will be assimilated and your progress will continue.

Motivation

It is easy to be motivated when you find yourself catching a rival, lap by lap. However, there will be times, particularly during endurance races, where you may be 'alone' on the track for long periods of time, with only your data logger and (potentially) your team manager on the radio to keep you going. Learning to motivate yourself during these moments

is critical to maintaining consistent, fast and error-free laps. This is when practicing techniques to hold your concentration can also help.

If there are no competitors in sight, set yourself goals with regards to backmarkers, aiming to catch one within a certain number of laps, or another at a specific point on the track. They're just little tricks to keep your performance level up. Chasing lap times isn't quite the same and as such is ill advised, however, because for many people it can prove counter-intuitive. The pressure of attempting to beat a specific time can shift the focus away from trying to perform at the best of your ability and you'll actually end up going round in a slower time because you're too preoccupied with the fact that every little imperfection is costing you precious thousandths of a second.

Luck

It is important to realise and accept that luck plays a major role in motorsport. Sometimes you'll be lucky, sometime you won't. You have to take it as part of the package and remain pragmatic when unfortunate things that are beyond your control happen. You can't do anything to change them so there's little point dwelling on them – accept it and move on.

Positivity

It is often said that negativity and a defeatist outlook can severely hinder a driver's performance. It's easy for beginners, for instance, to find themselves behind another kart and convince themselves that they will never be able to overtake it. Or, if they fall off the track, believe that they will never master the necessary racecraft.

Good business managers will motivate their team with a pep talk. A very simple but extremely effective technique, and the best thing is that it works even when it is self-administered. Giving yourself a pep talk while you're out on the track can wipe away the negative thoughts, allow you to regain focus and bring yourself back into contention.

Look ahead

Don't ever look behind you. There's no better way to lose your focus or spur on a pursuing competitor than to turn round to see how far behind you they

are on the track. Even if it's not the case and you're perfectly in control of your situation, their interpretation will inevitably be that they've got you worried over their presence and that it is now only a matter of time before they catch and eventually pass you. That will usually boost their performance and, as they close in, undoubtedly affect yours.

With experience you'll get to the point of hearing or even feeling another kart following closely behind but until then you can use little tricks such as taking

ABOVE Don't look behind you – focus on the road ahead instead. *(Darren Bourne)*

OPPOSITE It's important to accept that luck plays a significant part in racing. *(Enver Meyer)*

LEFT If you really must, choose a point on the track that enables a discreet peak behind you. *(Enver Meyer)*

note of shadows, when racing during late afternoon or in winter. Another way is to notice the direction of the gaze of a rival team manager as they hold their driver's pit board, to indicate the presence of another kart. As for keeping an eye on a closing competitor, if you must, tracks will often offer opportunities through their design (eg hairpins) to get a sneak peak at what's going on behind you without giving anything away. Alternatively, look for that information on your own pit board or hear it through your radio communication system.

The crucial aspect to remember is to not waste mental effort thinking about what is happening behind you. Concentrate on what you can control by maximising your driving and only focus on your defensive lines when you absolutely need to. Until then, you should be worrying about what's ahead of you and making sure your driving is as clean and accurate as it can be.

Clear the air

All drivers at some point will face some altercation on-track. Perhaps someone has cut them off when they felt they had the corner. Or they've been unceremoniously bumped off the circuit by an overzealous competitor. The scenarios are as varied as the excuses you'll hear from the offending party, but it is important to deal with these straight after the race. This doesn't mean going over to punch the culprit as soon as he gets back to the pits, of course. But it does mean having a polite yet stern word with the individual – it's usually enough to stop them from doing it again should you ever both find each other in the same situation.

Earlier in the book, driving etiquette is discussed and while you should obviously be considerate towards fellow competitors, you should obviously always stand your ground when necessary (and this may include having to deal with a certain

driver's on-track antics in the most appropriate manner). As mentioned earlier, part of the racing occurs before you even get in the kart. How other drivers regard you off the track will affect the way they react to you on it, so it is important to not to let others walk over you and firmly establish yourself as a genuine contender.

Get a visor

When buying your helmet, purchase a tinted visor at the same time. Clear visors are useful for dusk and night-time driving, of course, but at any other time they allow every other competitor to see your current state of mind. A racing lid's aperture may not be wide, but you'd be surprised at how easy it is to read a driver's mental state from just their eyes, particularly if they are a rookie racer. A tinted visor not only makes it impossible for competitors to make an assessment over your 'track status', it should also help with your confidence by providing a comforting psychological barrier. It is the exact same principle behind the fact so many celebrities wear sunglasses. (A dark visor also has other advantages, such as helping with practising visualisation techniques while on the starting grid without feeling self-conscious.)

Appearance

Often, new drivers will feel intimidated by a competitor who turns up with sponsor's decals plastered all over their suit, and go so far as to assume he must possess superior experience and driving skills. Sometimes that may be true, of course, but until you've been up against them on the track you won't know for certain. Company logo patches are easier to buy and get sewn on to a suit than they are to earn as a result on-track performance – don't assume a driver's ability (whether good or bad) simply from their appearance.

It's a similar approach with regards to a competitor's equipment. A shiny, brand-new kart with the latest and greatest parts on it isn't an indication of the driver's skill. It may simply be a rookie with more money than sense. You should judge your competitors on the track, not in the paddock.

Having said that, there's nothing to stop you taking advantage of how others may perceive you. After all, it is not unusual to see beginners in arrive-and-drive series get easily pressured by a competitor who is wearing his own suit and helmet and who comes up to pass them. The effect is less pronounced as you progress up the karting series, granted, but the fundamentals remain, meaning that your appearance will almost always have an effect on those around you. So it would be silly not to exploit this.

Besides, there is another advantage to focusing on your appearance. Karters will often openly admit that 'looking the part' makes them drive faster. There is some truth in that claim, and it can be explained by the way that you perceive yourself. Looking fast has the psychological effect of making you feel fast – it's effectively a simple way of boosting your confidence, and if you're confident, you'll invariably be performing at a higher level, meaning better driving and faster lap times.

Driver coaching

There is often a perception amongst drivers that racing ability is either genetically built into you or acquired in some imperceptible manner through track time. Clearly practice helps immensely, but if all you're doing is practising the wrong things, how far can you realistically expect to get? And what happens when you reach your 'maximum' – how do you progress then?

The answer is with driver coaching. If your ego is reeling at that sentence, don't let it – even 100m Olympic sprinters have coaches, and all they have to do is run, a capability most people develop in their early years. No one is born holding a kart, however.

A kart coaching programme will aim to improve your driving technique, remove bad habits and generally look to reduce your lap times by analysing your strengths and weaknesses, of course, but with particular relevance to this chapter are the psychological benefits that such an approach can have. Driver development is as much about the mind as it is the driving, and a coach will work hard to strengthen areas such as confidence, concentration and motivation. It's by no means the cheapest solution, but it could fast-track you to a level of competition you may never reach if left to your own devices.

LEFT Don't be taken in by appearances: judge drivers by their on-track performance. *(Enver Meyer)*

8

Strategy

Introduction

In the same way that Napoleon would have been unlikely to have won wars without any planning, you are unlikely to win races without good strategy. The race itself is obviously the event that all the focus is on, but it is actually only the last session in a sequence that is necessary to guarantee racing success. Before the race there is much work to undertake in terms of testing, practice and qualifying, with each session requiring its own approach.

There are tactical elements that apply to all, however. For instance, it's good practice to get into the habit of writing a list of equipment needed for each session to ensure you don't forget to take anything with you. And while we're on the subject of lists, good documentation is a crucial element of a successful kart team. Regardless of the session, always note down every set-up change, driving lines tried, temperatures, tyre pressures, times, handling descriptions. You'll be surprised how much you can learn with regards to the nature and characteristics of your kart once you start to review your notes from various test or race meetings. Suddenly, working out set-up changes becomes a far more straightforward and intuitive process.

You should also get into the habit of checking the weather forecast. This is particularly crucial for endurance events. Several internet sites offer excellent reports, including satellite imagery so that you can assess the situation as accurately as possible and plan your strategy accordingly.

Testing

Many circuits offer testing sessions throughout the week. If possible, aim to attend these as the track is likely to be a lot calmer, ensuring a better environment in which to get your work done, particularly if you are just starting out.

Consistency

Until you are driving consistently, testing is primarily a way of getting experience and invaluable track time. There is no point fooling around with settings until you know that you can rely on your driving to accurately indicate whether, say, it is the increased camber that has made you faster or it is the fact that you're now braking two metres deeper into the bottom hairpin. Initially, concentrate on your driving and closely monitor your performance on the track to ensure you are not developing (and practicing) any bad habits. Once you are lapping consistently, then it's time to start experimenting with new lines and set-up changes.

Equally, there is an argument for knowing a track intimately in order to test different set-ups consistently, but this should not stop you from testing at a track you are still learning. If nothing else, it is the perfect opportunity to try to perfect a corner that's been causing you difficulty.

Don't overdo it

Use testing properly. Too often competitors will meet on the track during testing and get a little carried away. Testing is not a race, so don't get sucked into racing other karts which can often end with someone going off the track and damaging their equipment. Hardly an ideal situation if you're close to race day and you haven't got any spares.

Similarly, know when to stop. If you're there for track time, then obviously maximise the opportunity, but if you're testing for set-up before a race then once you have found what you believe to be the ultimate pace then make a note of it and pack up. There's little point in overstressing components and putting needless miles on the chassis chasing an extra thousandth of a second or two.

Test the right equipment

It is obviously important to test as close to race conditions as possible. This means any equipment you use, such as radio kit, ballast, neck brace and

OPPOSITE Consistent success in races comes from a professional approach to karting.
(Enver Meyer)

BELOW The key to good testing is to be consistent and systematic.
(Darren Bourne)

so on, should be worn to emulate the real race situation. This extends to the tyres, too. Testing for set-up on old tyres is not constructive. You may find a quick setting that then alters significantly once you put on fresh rubber because of the different handling characteristics these bring with them.

Be methodical

When making set-up changes it is crucial to make one change at any one time. Otherwise you won't be able to work out which change has made the kart faster (or slower). Make a tweak, get out on the track, time your laps, come back into pits. Remember to make a note of the set-up, lap times, track conditions, weather, temperature (atmospheric, track and tyres), tyre pressures and so on.

Finally, many teams waste an awful of time when testing due to a lack of organisation. Have a plan of the set-ups you want to try or what you hope to achieve during the session. This will help you stay focused on your task.

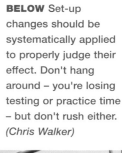

BELOW Set-up changes should be systematically applied to properly judge their effect. Don't hang around – you're losing testing or practice time – but don't rush either. *(Chris Walker)*

Practice

In many series, practice occurs on race day and time is at a premium. Your kart should therefore be fully prepped and ready to hit the track as soon as you get to the circuit.

Race pace

Practice differs from testing in that the pace on the track should match the intensity of the racing session. Partly because it helps you get into the right frame of mind but also due to the fact you'll need to set up the kart for qualifying. With regards to the latter, you should therefore be practising on near-qualifying settings so you maximise your performance when it comes to putting in a quick lap. It is important to know the limits of new tyres, for example, particularly if your series runs a short stint qualifying structure requiring you to be on the pace from the moment you leave the pits. If you've never practised working out the limitations of your equipment in qualifying trim, then you just won't know how hard to push during

qualifying itself. It is also important to be aware of just how late you can brake with your current set-up and tyres, crucial information for when attempting to overtake the competition.

Be concise
Given the typically short sessions, don't stay out on track too long – once you've worked out the kart's characteristics that need tweaking, come in, make the change, and get out again.

Know the track
Once you're happy with your set-up and have time, use it to try different lines to find out grip levels when attempting to overtake, for instance. If you haven't ventured off the racing line, doing so first time in the race in order to pass a competitor could have some unexpected and potentially race-ruining consequences. It is always better to be launching yourself into familiar territory, whenever possible.

Learn from others
Lastly, don't spend all of your practice time focused solely on your team and kart. Keep an eye on what everyone else is doing. Time the quick competitors, and if you're in a friendly, not overly competitive series chat to them about chassis set-up, tyre pressures, and so on. This isn't F1 so don't expect the same secrecy – most experienced karters are usually happy to help out beginners and most classes have a friendly club spirit.

Qualifying

In any category of motorsport, where you start in a race is important, of course, but with a class so closely fought as karting, it becomes fundamental towards ensuring potential success. This is certainly true in sprint events, where you can lose precious laps trying to get past competitors you could have had starting behind you by out-qualifying them. In endurance events it's somewhat less of an issue because there's usually plenty time to get past drivers and you can make up valuable time with carefully orchestrated pit stops, for instance.

Format strategy
It is important to find out the format of qualifying so you can set up your kart and your strategy accordingly. Whether it's run over one lap, five laps, or for 15 minutes, it all makes a difference. With tenths of a second having a genuine effect on your overall position, think about elements other than settings (which should have been finalised during

practice) that will give you a performance edge. For instance, consider the level of fuel you're carrying because as long as you come in above the minimum weight regulation there is no need to take extra weight in the form of unnecessary fuel on to the track and lose precious time.

If it's a short qualifying run, you won't have time for the tyres to come up to temperature so think about increasing the pressure to accelerate the process and simulate race temperature pressure. You can work out how much additional pressure to put in by simulating a one or two-lap run during practice and checking the pressure when you come off the track against that of running for several laps at ideal race pressure. And remember to clean your tyres. New rubber picks up all sorts of rubbish and while the racing line is relatively clean, the pit area probably won't be.

If the qualifying session features several karts on the track at once, make sure you find yourself space to get a clear run by speeding up or slowing down to build a gap. The last thing you want is to have your lap time ruined by coming up behind a kart as you're in the middle to the end of a timed run.

Timing
If you have a choice, time your outing well. The track should already be fairly clean from the practice runs but letting a few competitors out first could ensure a little extra grip as more rubber gets laid down from the new tyres they're likely to

ABOVE Karting grids can be large, so maximising your qualifying performance is particularly crucial – notice the difference in distance from the front to the rear of the grid. *(Chris Walker)*

ABOVE Capitalising on opportunities during starts takes plenty of experience.
(Enver Meyer)

OPPOSITE TOP Remember starts offer the highest risk of silly accidents.
(Enver Meyer)

OPPOSITE BOTTOM It's always a good habit to observe the races you're not involved in.
(Enver Meyer)

be running. However, keep an eye on the weather. If it looks as though the temperature is likely to drop or there's rain on the way, then obviously get out and put a time in as early as possible.

Approach

Drivers who practice visualisation techniques or have a routine in place to enable them to get out on to the track and be immediately on the pace are obviously at an advantage when it comes to qualifying. Until you're at a similar level, you'll have to approach this session as best as your ability will allow. It is obviously crucial to be quick, but a mistake many beginners make is to overdrive their kart. This actually ends up costing them time, as well as damaging their set of tyres, which they are likely to need for the race.

If you do have had a bad qualifying round, don't torment yourself by dwelling on it. Work out a different strategy for improving your chances from your current position instead. You should aim to keep a positive attitude at all times.

Race start

Undoubtedly, the best time of a race to gain the most number of places is at the start. But it is also the most chaotic, dangerous and potentially nerve-racking moment, requiring extreme concentration, level headedness, great peripheral awareness, ruthless opportunism, quick reactions, and experience.

Aggression

The race start requires you to be aggressive and defensive at all times, and to not let yourself be intimidated by other drivers. You should be in the right state of mind to be able to cope with this. A karting acquaintance once suggested shouting at yourself as you're going round the track during the formation lap. If it works for you, use it (but try not to let the marshals hear you or they'll think you've lost it).

Of course, being 'aggressive' doesn't mean driving competitors off the track, but you shouldn't allow yourself to be pushed around either. Stand your ground. Your primary objective should be to hold your position and once that is assured, you should then focus on gaining positions. Obviously, within the confusion of a race start, this doesn't tend to work out quite as systematically, but you'll get the idea.

Spotting opportunities

Look well ahead. As already mentioned, if karts in front of you tangle, try to spot a gap as early as possible. This may mean running off the track, which isn't ideal but remains a preferable alternative to running into the side of a stationary kart, of course.

Generally, the most chaotic place to be during a race start is in the midfield and it's not unusual to get bounced around like a pinball for the first couple of corners. It's actually a very quick way to gain a great deal of experience. By comparison, starting from the back is far less stressful and can offer the most opportunity to pick up a decent number of positions because you're well placed to judge what is going on ahead. Conversely, starting at the front requires you to go on the defensive from the moment the lights go green and can be a very tense place to be for a beginner karter. But, again, it's experience you wouldn't do without.

It pays to watch other starts to see any potential first corner patterns that you may be able to exploit. There is one particular track in the UK with a wide right hander which the majority of competitors bunch up and hug the inside at the start of a race, meaning you can drive around the outside and pick up a ridiculous number of positions.

ABOVE Even at the highest level, rolling starts can prove unfair – the accepted rule is that as soon as the guys in front hit the throttle, you do the same. *(Enver Meyer)*

Rolling starts

For rolling starts, it is important to keep alongside your rival as you go around the track for the formation lap. While still in the pits waiting to go out, make a mental note of the karts in front as well as alongside so you'll know your position should you get out of formation once out on the track. Try to keep a constant distance to the kart ahead and to the side of you but if the guy in front is dropping back, a gentle nudge should help them get their focus back.

Be aware that the formation lap may take a shorter route than the full circuit to cut out any hairpins that can cause two-stroke engines to oil up and bog down when in a slow formation queue-type situation.

Warm up the kart and clear the engine by opening up the throttle on your way on to the track. Keeping your foot on the brake will warm up the disc, while weaving to warm up tyres actually

makes very little difference and is not allowed at some clubs. It is better to concentrate on powering around corners and speeding up and slowing down on straights to increase friction and therefore heat.

While on the formation lap be aware of what is happening. Get confirmation in advance of how many rolling laps are planned and keep an eye on the grid – if it's in reasonably good order, the start is likely to happen on that lap. Maintain a little pressure on the brake so you can be on the throttle and increase the revs slightly without the kart speeding up. Keep an eye on the marshal on the start line and don't get caught sleeping – floor the accelerator as soon those in front do the same. Waiting for the flag or light signal is theoretically correct but doing so could see you languishing behind as everyone else takes off. By their very nature, rolling starts are a little inconsistent at best so the rule is to do

whatever everyone else is doing as long as it's not a blatant jump start. (Note that you're not usually allowed to overtake until you've passed the start/finish line though, again, not everyone abides by this rule.)

Watch out for first corner bunch ups, avoid colliding with competitors and keep an eye out for spinning karts and try to drive around them. The sooner you settle into a rhythm, the better, although this may take a few corners as everyone falls into place.

Standing starts

Getting good momentum build up off the line is the hardest part of a standing start. To help matters, a little throttle just before the lights go green is acceptable as long as you don't burn the clutch – don't blip the throttle, just a little pressure on the pedal will help raise the revs enough to hopefully give you an advantage.

As soon as the lights change, you're free to floor the throttle. Some drivers assist the kart to get going by jumping forward to help the engine pick up. Bear in mind most clubs won't allow any overtaking until you've passed the start/finish line and will usually force the karts either side of a row of cones (this is also usual practice for rolling starts). Be aware of this, if so, and instantly move into a defensive (or attacking) position once you've cleared the line.

It's worth noting which side of the track you will be starting from. The 'clean' side is the one over which the racing runs, whereas the 'dirty' side is the area of the start/finish straight that doesn't see much action. As a result, it tends to be more prone to dirt than tyre rubber deposit, meaning it can offer considerably less grip. Depending on the class of kart you are racing, this will have a varying degree of effect – for many classes the performance drop may well be negligible.

The race

Assuming you've survived the start unscathed, you'll now want to focus on the race itself. The strategy for this, it may not surprise you to hear, is usually pretty straightforward and simply involves the need to drive as fast and as consistent as you possibly can.

Whatever you do, never, ever give up and back off your pace. Accidents and mechanical failures can happen to your competitors, or the weather may change, and you need to be in the best placed position to capitalise on this. And the best position to be is as close as you can to them, meaning you need to keep driving as fast as you're able to. In addition, keeping competitors under pressure may force them into mistakes so you should keep pushing until you pass the chequered flag. The only permissible time you should ever consider slowing down your pace is as a result of a mechanical problem and the need to nurse the kart home to the finish line, and hopefully some well-earned championship points.

Sprint

With the short number of laps of most sprint heats, you can't afford to hang about. Passing must be decisive and brave. Try not to fall into the rhythm of the competitor in front, which is easily done, and waste two or three laps caught up behind them.

Good, consistent finishes in the heats will guarantee you a decent starting position for the final so think about the consequences of attempting a dangerous pass that you don't manage to pull off – you would end up losing a lot of places (and could even fail to finish). It may be smarter to hold on to your current position and try to make up the places in the final. You can also save the do-or-die overtaking attempts for then, when you know there are no more rounds left in the day.

Endurance

It is often said that you can't win an endurance on the first lap but you can definitely lose it. This it true, although it obviously doesn't mean you shouldn't be pushing as hard as you can from the moment the race starts – if you've ever watched an endurance event you will have noticed the drivers aren't exactly Sunday driving their way around the track. The top teams will be racing hard from start to finish and there is usually surprisingly little between them even after several hours. But there is a different mentality to endurance events and the focus is more on consistency than simply outright speed. Often, the winning team is not the one with the fastest laps, but the one that didn't fall off the track, planned its driver changes and fuel stops intelligently, and had great reliability due to good prepping.

Further to the concept of consistency in the race, is consistency between team mates. This is crucial. If you have a team made up of decent

drivers with say only, half a second a lap difference between them then you'll be in a much stronger position than the team that has one very quick racer but two that are one and half seconds off the pace.

When racing as a team, too many beginner drivers stick religiously to equal stints for each of the various team members. The thing to realise is that you have to be flexible for the good of the race. Sure, everyone has paid so they should theoretically all get same track time, but if you're planning on winning it may be necessary to extend the time of one particular driver or even keep another one out of the seat altogether. Everyone has their off days, and certain circuits will suit certain drivers better than others so it is important to monitor your team member's individual performances and make tactical decisions based on how the race is evolving.

You will need to have contingency plans in place and pre-empt any potential problems such as punctures by having spares ready (tyres mounted on rims and at the correct pressure) in the pit area. The time you save as a result of being proactive about most potential technical and mechanical issues can be massive. The right preparation means you're less likely to be caught out when or if something goes wrong.

Related to this is the need to have elements

such as all wet-weather set-up gear in a separate container so it's all in one place for an easy change over should it suddenly start raining. Again, remember to have the correct tyre pressures already set to save time.

Coming into the pits underweight can be a genuine threat for many endurance teams. Often, drivers forget to take the season and weather into account. When doing long stints of over an hour during a hot summer's day, for example, it is not unusual for a driver to lose a few kilos through sweating which could make the difference between being above the minimum limit, or under it. Another issue is the fact that you'll obviously want to minimise the number of refuelling stops and will therefore run for as long as possible. This is fine, as long as you factor in the loss of weight into your calculations. Typically, the penalty for coming in underweight is severe (being docked ten laps is not uncommon) and not something you can make up by getting back out on to the track and giving it everything you've got, no matter how good a driver you are.

Last but by no means least, you need a team manager who oversees the tactical side of the race and makes strategic decisions with regards to pit stops, driver changes, and tyre choice, to name three. Drivers should ideally be focused on the racing and nothing else.

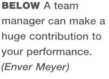

BELOW A team manager can make a huge contribution to your performance. *(Enver Meyer)*

Pit strategy

While much of this following section is of primary interest to endurance racers, the organisational aspects certainly apply to all classes of karting.

Be as efficient as you can in the pits. It's advisable to duplicate certain tools as you'll need them simultaneously not only during set-up but, crucially, in race pit stops if repairs or settings changes are needed. Organise your tools in the same manner at each meeting so you know where to look for everything and can find what you need quickly. At the end of the race, packing everything away in its correct place will obviously speed up the process at the following meeting.

Learn the sizes of bolts, screws and nuts that hold your kart together. This saves a massive amount of time during repair pit stops and can also come into play in terms of getting the right tools ready should a driver communicate a problem for which they are having to come back into the pits.

If you don't have radio communication, work out in advance simple signals that may refer to trouble in different areas of the kart, such as engine, steering, wheels/tyres, chassis and so on.

ABOVE Efficiency and organisation in the pits is crucial. *(Darren Bourne)*

LEFT Radio communication is becoming increasingly common in karting, certainly for endurance rounds, and strategically can prove invaluable. *(Enver Meyer)*

OPPOSITE The racing
doesn't stop during a
pit stop – you should
work hard to minimise
the time lost in the pits.
(Darren Bourne)

Time refuelling stops properly so that the fuel
bay is empty when your kart comes in, eradicating
the amount of time you would have lost sitting
behind another kart while it is being refuelled. This
may sometimes mean having to wait for several
laps as most teams come in to refuel around the
same time so plan this into your strategy – you'll
need the ability to run for longer if need be, and do
so without running out of fuel or coming in
underweight. One approach to help avoid this
stressful situation is to run a slightly different
strategy with regards to fuel so that you're either
side of the main refuelling window, thereby
maximising your chances of finding an empty fuel
bay when you do come in.

Organise driver changes and refuelling pit stops
by assigning a specific role to each team member.
Someone should focus on taking ballast off (or
adding it on), someone else should tighten the
fuel cap back and/or lube the chain, while a third
re-starts the engine(s).

Practice this, along with the more common
repair issues such as wheel and body panel
changes resulting from race damage, as well as the
kind of set-up alterations you may need, given the
changing conditions of the track.

Above all, remain calm and collected. Running
around shouting frantically, aside from potentially
earning you a penalty, will do little to get the kart
back out on the track as quickly as possible.

Finally, never underestimate the importance of a
good pit stop. The time you save from a quick,
carefully executed stop can amount to tens of
seconds over the competition, the kind of
advantage you would never make up on the
track given a closely matched field. Take it as
seriously as the racing itself because it is part of the
same package. Winning endurance teams are not
always the fastest at the meeting, but they do tend
to be the most organised. Sloppy pit stops will lose
you races, regardless of how good your drivers
may be.

BELOW Being
organised and well
drilled will save you
invaluable time
during a pit stop.
(Greg Richardson)

Technicalities

Introduction

In reality, it would be easy to fill a book when dealing with the intricacies of a kart's set-up. Much of the content would be things you will pick up as you start racing and tinkering with your kart. It's safe to say that almost every decision you make on a kart, from the wheel choice to where you place your hands when steering, has an effect on handling. With changing technologies, the differences in chassis behaviour, the specific characteristics of each track and countless other potential permutations, you're unlikely to ever stop learning.

Trying out new set-ups and gaining time is an enjoyable part of the process as long as you accept that the biggest improvement you can make to a kart is adding a good driver. So in that sense, as with all the other elements covered so far, technicalities such as set-up are just part of the overall bundle. While the following is by no means a comprehensive lesson, what you'll find here are some basics to start you off on your journey to be the most complete driver you can hope to be.

Chassis

While all kart chassis adhere to the same overriding unsprung, straightforward tubular design, there is actually great variety within the models available. Ultimately, they are intended to perform the same function but some will naturally suit the power requirements and format of certain categories, as well as the driving characteristics of some drivers, more than others. As with any other part, the chassis deteriorates with usage and will need replacing once its properties have diminished through wear and stress.

Flex

Beginner drivers will often seem a little incredulous when an experienced driver mentions the flexibility of a chassis, possibly finding it difficult to accept that the apparently very stiff kart they are sitting in would actually twist as different forces are applied on it from going around a track. But it is worth remembering that it is precisely due to the fact that a kart does not feature suspension that chassis are designed to flex. As mentioned previously, you wouldn't get them to go around corners if they didn't. Their whole design is based around the principle of being able to lift the inside rear wheel in order to get the chassis to pivot rather than stubbornly hurtle off the track in a straight line.

The variety in flex from chassis to chassis usually affects how long and how quickly the inside rear tyre will lift (the more flex, the longer the lift), but flex can often be further adjusted with the addition or removal of a variety of torsion bars and rails. Also worth experimenting with is the loosening of either the front or rear bumper when more flex in the chassis is required.

Rear axle

Available in a range of materials and diameters, not many new drivers realise rear axles can also affect handling. They are usually labelled soft, medium and stiff. Using the latter will increase the rear traction levels by transferring more load to the rear tyres and is beneficial at circuits which provide little grip. Conversely, the softer option reduces rear traction and is necessary in situations where there is plenty of grip available. Medium is a good compromise between the two and one of the reasons it is a popular choice.

Choosing a chassis

Deciding on which chassis to get is one of those things that can be as much fun as it is infuriating. They're not cheap and it is obviously a commitment that forces you down a certain route that may or may not be the right one for you. As mentioned in Chapter 2, choosing something that is winning across a variety of championships rather than just your local series (so that it is more likely to be a true reflection of the chassis's ability rather than that of a very talented driver) is a good bet, as is the opportunity to try out as many on your short list as possible.

Also worth considering is selecting a make that is not only stocked by your local karting retailer but, more importantly, that is also used by other drivers in the series you plan to compete in. This will help with set-up, maintenance and repair advice by talking to the other teams, but also in terms of getting access to spares should you unexpectedly need to replace a part you haven't got but another team is happy to sell or loan to you until you can get your own. It sounds improbable – and certainly in the higher, more serious series it is an unlikely scenario – but at many levels of karting the feeling of community and the assistance you get from other team members is enough to make you believe in the possibility of World peace. With that in mind, if there's several of you running the same chassis, organising bulk orders can be a cost-effective way of buying new equipment.

The last point to make about buying a new chassis is to consider waiting for the latest version. Keep an eye on manufacturers' websites, karting forums and magazines for any announcements relating to this. Chassis technology is continually improving and it would be silly to spend your money on last year's model if there's a new one about to be released.

Set-up

Elements of set-up have been mentioned in other areas of the book, so the purpose here is to detail some of the remaining main points that you ought to be familiar with.

Baseline set-up

This is your set-up reference and is kart which is as near balanced and neutral handling as you can make it, and from which you can most accurately judge the effect of changes to settings that you make. Unless you're making progress when tinkering, you should return to the baseline set-up, the settings for which you should have recorded. As already mentioned, this holds true for any set-up change. The more information you have, the quicker you'll grasp the fundamentals of configuring your kart's handling ability. So get into the habit of using a set-up sheet to keep track of the set-ups you've tried.

Tyres and set-up

One way to throw money away is to use a new set of tyres every time the kart is taken out on to the track. It's perfectly fine to start setting up your kart by going out on the tyres you used in the previous meeting, set a good baseline set-up and then work towards your qualifying set-up. This is when you can use your new set of tyres, to get your kart as high up

Kart set-up sheet

a. Toe-in/out	R		L	
b. Camber/Caster	R		L	
c. Front spacing	R		L	
d. Rear spacing	R		L	
e. Sprocket size				
f. Rim size	Ft		Rr	
g. Tyre size	Ft		Rr	
h. Tyre pressure	Ft		Rr	
i. Ballast	L		R	
j. Stiffener bar				
k. Seat position/type				

Driver:

Time:

Track temp:

Peak RPM:

Tyres:

Air temp:

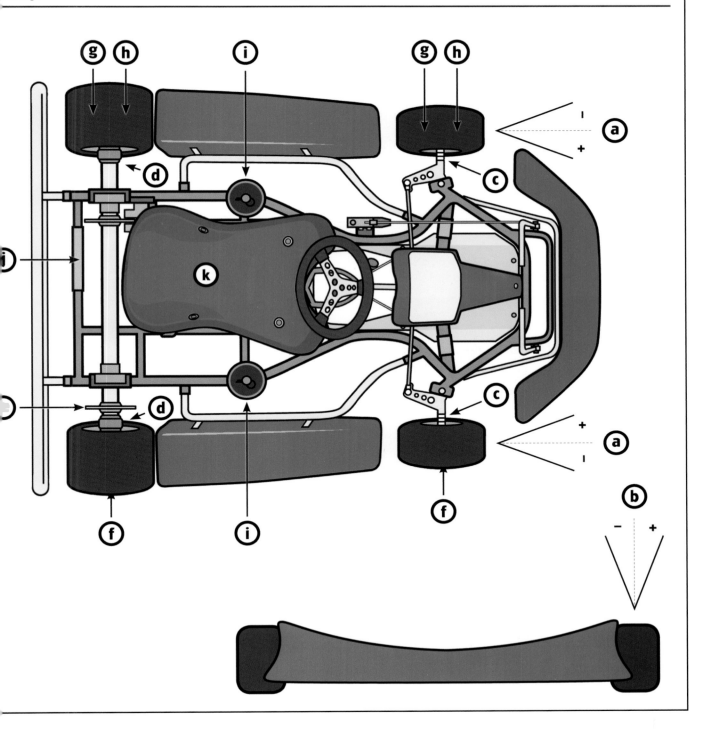

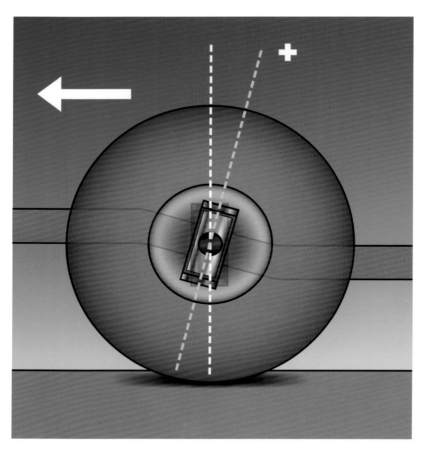

the grid as your equipment and skill will allow.

Remember that a qualifying set-up and race set-up are not the same thing. In real terms, it's better to have a great set-up on worn tyres than one that's geared specifically for new tyres – you'll spend most of the day on worn tyres, after all.

Caster

Caster helps keep a kart from wandering in a straight line due to the torque value created by the difference between the angle of the spindle in relation to an imaginary vertical line running through the wheel. The greater the caster angle, the more difficult it becomes to turn the wheel. But as discussed in Chapter 4, caster also assists in getting a kart around corners. The more steering lock you apply, the more the inside wheel is forced against the track surface, and the more the outside wheel rises. Because you're going round a corner, the chassis naturally drops on to the outside wheel, which in turn helps unload the inside rear tyre, thereby allowing the kart to rotate. Caster shouldn't normally be altered unless other adjustments are having no effect on steering responsiveness.

Caster is fundamental to enabling a kart to turn by allowing the inside rear wheel to lift.

Camber

This works in conjunction with caster to help a kart change direction quickly and in a capable fashion. Camber can be described as the vertical inclination affecting the front wheels. When looking at the front of the kart, negative camber is seen on a wheel sloping towards the kart, while positive camber will have the wheel leaning towards the outside of the kart. Its purpose is to maximise the tyre's contact patch during cornering and will enable you to alter a front wheel that is running predominantly on the tyre's outside or inside edge, so that it adopts the correct angle for the tyre to work flat against the track.

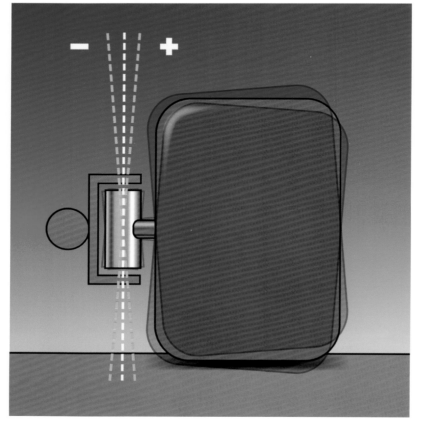

Camber represents the amount of 'lean' applied to the wheel and affects the tyre's contact patch during cornering.

Toe

Toe refers to the difference in distance between the front and the rear of the directional tyres. Most karts use zero toe, meaning the front wheels are parallel to each other, or fractional toe-in (the wheels point inwards at one another). Toe-out is used during wet races, when turn-in needs to be exaggerated and the resulting scrubbing keeps the tyres at a better operating temperature, thereby increasing grip. Toe settings are usual minimal due to the resulting loss of speed through excessive scrubbing, and are worked out after camber and caster have been set (as these affect the toe value).

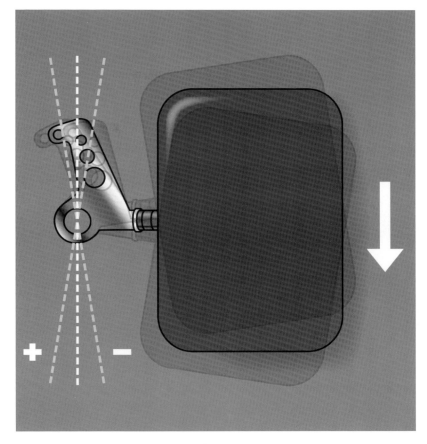

Toe-in primarily affects straightline stability, while toe-out improves turn-in ability.

Seat

When you consider the fact that the seat holds the most ballast – the driver – then it is reasonably obvious to expect its position to have possibly the biggest impact on how the kart will handle itself on the track. Seat manufacturers often lecture at karting exhibitions and can spend an hour only scratching the surface of seat dynamics. It's not simply that the seat's position has an effect on the weight distribution, the weight transfer and the centre of gravity, but how even tiny changes to these then go on to interact with all the other elements of handling, and how intricate and significant this relationship can turn out to be. This is one of the reasons why drivers who use ballast should ideally try to secure the weight on the actual seat rather than the typical mounting poles either side of the kart.

The easiest advice to give is to follow your chassis manufacturer's recommendation for the positioning of the seat. This is the one most likely to have the best perspective on this, after all, having tested every variation with regards to driver size, weight, tyre choice and circuit type.

The last point is important, as ideally you will want to set up your seat position depending on the characteristics of the track, and then build the rest

LEFT Seat positioning is one of the most crucial set-up changes you can make on a kart. *(Enver Meyer)*

of the set-up around this. In this respect, endurance teams are at a disadvantage and the likelihood of finding a position that perfectly suits both the track and all team members is remote, unless the latter are all physically identical. Assuming this is not the case, a compromise will have to be found.

Regardless of where and how the seat ends up, ensure that you are sitting snugly in position as you're racing around. It is important to get the correct-sized seat to stop the unnecessary (and handling-destroying) effect of the weight transfer of a driver who is loose inside the seat. Equally, all fixings should be checked for tightness, for precisely the same reason, and don't forget to consider the different levels of seat stiffness available as this will act on the amount of influence you have over chassis flex.

Tyres

As already discussed in Chapter 4, tyres are the most crucial component of a kart's handling, and can therefore have one of the greatest effects on your performance – either positively or otherwise. So it becomes imperative to take the time to learn as much about their characteristics as possible, as well as how to correctly look after them both on and off the track.

Always remember that tyres require temperature in order to provide traction. A common rookie mistake is to blast out of the pits on cold tyres, get to the braking zone of the first corner at normal racing speed and unceremoniously find themselves running or spinning off the track. Depending on the compound, it may take several laps before tyres reach their correct operating temperature. Only then can you be thinking about going around at the usual race speed and sticking to the usual braking points. When you first venture out on to the track you should always be prepared to tiptoe around some of the corners.

Compounds

The majority of karting series will usually have a designated dry and wet tyre which competitors must adhere to in order to compete in the championship. The need for such control becomes obvious when you consider that just a change in tyre compound – how hard or soft the tyre's rubber is – can have a dramatic influence on handling.

A hard compound provides less grip and requires a high operating temperature but has longevity in its favour, making it the ideal choice for endurance events. By contrast, soft tyres offer far

better traction, operate at a lower temperature (and therefore start performing earlier than their hard compound counterparts), but wear out far sooner, making them only suited to sprint meetings.

Heat cycle

Every time you go out on to the track and stop back in the pits, your tyres will have warmed up to race temperature and then cooled back down to ambient temperature. That is one heat cycle. The more cycles you put a tyre through, the more traction it loses as the oils in the rubber evaporate, and the harder it gets. Eventually, it becomes time to put on a new set. On harder compounds, heat cycles have less effect and the tyre will perform more evenly, offering similar levels of grip throughout most of its lifespan. Softer tyres don't fare as well, and show signs of degradation after just very few cycles.

Storage

New tyres come wrapped in plastic. Unless you are about to drive on your brand-new set of boots, keep them in their original packaging which is preserving the oils in the rubber and which degrade when in contact with air and UV light.

It is also important to keep new tyres in an environment that doesn't suffer from a wide temperature range. A garage, for instance, isn't a good idea because the day/night temperature changes will have a similar effect as putting a tyre through a heat cycle, meaning the rubber will be getting harder just by being sat in storage. Similarly, keeping them indoors but too close to a radiator or in an area where sunlight can reach them isn't going to do them any favours either. Try to find an area with as constant a temperature reading as possible.

Scrubbing in

If tyres deteriorate and lose their traction properties with heat cycles, then logically a new tyre will provide the most grip, won't it? Well, no. It will, but not until you've 'scrubbed' it in. While the highly slippery new sheen on the tyre surface is still present, the first couple of corners on new rubber is not unlike driving on butter. By the third corner, as this layer begins to disappear, the grip level increases. This does not mean you should power slide around the first bend as a way of accelerating the process – abusing the tyres on their first outing will ruin them immediately.

Instead, you should drive at a moderate pace around the track, gradually building the tyres up to race temperature, then run for three or so more laps before returning to the pits and letting the tyres

cool down. You should aim to get the tyres up to
operating temperature without racing around as
though you're on a qualifying stint. Be smooth, be
gentle and then bring them back in as soon as
you've completed the necessary laps. Following
this process is important because it allows the tyre
compound to stabilise, meaning the tyre is then
ready for anything you throw at it.

Reading the tyre

You should always check the condition of the tyres

when you come back into the pits and record your
findings. It may be an idea to invest in a tyre
temperature gauge and take readings across three
points (outside, middle and inside) on each of the
tyres. As well as using it to determine how 'flat' the
tyre is connecting to the track (and whether you
need to tweak your camber settings in order to
maximise the contact patch if the readings are
significantly different), the average of the three
readings will give you a more accurate temperature
value for each tyre. It is obviously important to do
this as soon as possible once the kart has come in
so as not to get a false reading as a result of the
tyres having had time to cool down.

Temperature is only half the story however, when
it comes to determining what the tyres have been
up to on the circuit. An experienced karter will know
from examining the wear pattern on the tyre surface
how well it is performing. Any sign of blistering, for
instance, and it is a good indication that the tyre is
overheating from having too much grip. If it gets too
hot, then it is likely to start disintegrating, which will
manifest itself through chunks of rubber missing
from the surface. You don't need experience to
realise that isn't necessarily a good sign.

Meanwhile, a tyre with too smooth a surface is
not generating enough heat and, as a
consequence, will lack grip.

What you want to be seeing is a tyre with a light grainy pattern and a dull surface finish. If that's not what your wear pattern looks like, then play around with pressures to try to sort out the problem.

Pressure

It is relatively easy for beginner drivers to get perplexed by tyre pressure, which is measured in psi, if only because it seems other drivers have a sixth sense about what setting to go for. The anxiety can be exacerbated by the fact that tyre pressure is critical in how it affects a kart's handling.

The first thing to note is that regardless of what pressure you start off with, by the time the kart returns to the pits the pressure will have gone up. This is because tyres generate heat when being driven, and heat causes the pressure to build up. So when you're working out your ideal pressure, take this inevitable increase into account. You can work out how much increase has occurred by taking a reading once the kart comes back into the pits after getting everything up to race temperature (remember not to hang around and give the tyres a chance to cool and therefore lose pressure), and compare this figure with your original setting.

Tyres do not warm up at consistent rates all-round so you should compensate accordingly. To give you an example, say you're running a Rotax Max in the UK on a right-hand circuit in the dry. The left rear tyre will work the hardest – meaning it will heat up the fastest – followed by the left front, and then the two tyres on the right. If you're aiming for a racing pressure of between 13-15psi, you should start by inflating the rear left to just 7psi, the front left to 8psi and 9psi on both rights. The kart will feel very heavy to drive but will improve as the tyres heat up and the pressure builds. Once they're hot, come in to the pits, let the tyres down to match the tyre with the lowest pressure and go out again to see how it feels. Repeat the process and you should end up with consistent hot pressures in all four tyres.

Clearly there are other elements such as track abrasiveness, tyre compound, class raced and so on to consider but the point is that it's always best to keep an open mind when it comes to tyre pressure. A set-up that feels undriveable can suddenly transform once the tyres are up to heat/pressure.

In addition, take the weather into account. Normally, as the ambient temperature increases, you ought to be decreasing the tyre pressure. This is because increased pressure increases the load on a tyre, meaning it will generate more grip but more heat, too. As the one thing you don't want is to have tyres that are overheating, so decrease the

Photo: *Enver Meyer*

Lastly, if you're hoping to counteract any oversteer or understeer issues by using pressure, then focus on the rear tyres only. Lowering the psi increases tyre wall flex (literally, how much of the side of the tyre flexes) which adds more back-end grip, thereby correcting an oversteering kart. When the grip at the back is pushing the front of the kart offline, in other words when it is understeering, increasing the pressure stiffens the tyre, which in turn reduces the amount of rear grip.

Wheels

Kart wheels are made of either aluminium or magnesium. Magnesium is both lighter and stiffer than aluminium but is also more fragile. Aluminium rims are therefore happier to withstand an impact (and hence recommended for beginners) and also flex more, meaning they will generally provide more tyre grip. This, of course, isn't always a desirable thing. Aside from the overheating effect it can have on a tyre, on lower powered karts too much grip will result in the karts bogging down and getting out of corners slower.

As well as coming in different materials, wheels also differ in width and this also affects the handling. Mounted on a narrower rim, the tyre will be taller and provide greater tyre sidewall flex and

ABOVE Despite proper prepping, certain components are highly stressed and can fail. *(Greg Richardson)*

BELOW Regular maintenance will keep the running costs down. *(Enver Meyer)*

pressure if the weather is getting hot. The tyres will still run at a decent temperature and produce good levels of traction, but the lower pressure will help reduce excessive heat generation.

Also consider the type of compound you are running. Harder tyres can cope with higher pressures than their softer equivalent because they don't generate heat as easily. So if you want to be guaranteed grip from hard tyres, you need to get some heat into them (but without overdoing it, clearly).

therefore more grip. On a wider wheel, the sidewall flex is obviously reduced as the tyre runs shorter on the rim, and as we have seen, a stiffer sidewall delivers less traction.

Maintenance and prep

Nothing lasts for ever, of course, and on a racing kart a number of elements undergo stressful and very short existences. If you're running on a tight budget obviously you'll have to accept compromises that may make it harder to win against better specced teams, but it certainly won't affect the fun you're having.

Nevertheless, even if you're not racing on a new chassis at every meeting, it is important to maintain your kart properly and there are specific areas that you'll want to focus on. Regular oil changes are relatively cheap but crucial, for instance, while inspecting your chain after each meeting is advisable. Your brakes are vital, arguably more so than your engine, so check the pads and the pedal travel. Also, keep an eye open for sheared wheel bearings, too – it's usually better to get a fresh set, and certainly if you're doing endurance rounds.

Those are just four examples. Ultimately, other

LEFT Regularly inspect components that suffer high levels of wear, such as sprockets. *(Enver Meyer)*

FAR LEFT Almost everything on a kart can be adjusted, including pedals. *(Enver Meyer)*

LEFT Mechanically, a kart is actually very simple – even specialised components soon become familiar. *(Enver Meyer)*

than the usual aspects that affect every driver, such as new tyres and engine rebuilds, how much maintenance your kart requires will also be down to your driving style. Some drivers who launch their karts over kerbs may need new stub axles at every race while someone with a gentler approach may get away with changing them every three meetings or so. Other than accidents, kerbs inevitably cause the biggest heartache, stressing components such as the chassis or even splitting the brake disc if you stray too far over. It pays to think about what you're doing on the track and having some mechanical sympathy for your kart, particularly if you're competing in long endurance races. Ultimately, remember you'll usually be the one to foot the bill.

Apart from looking after your equipment while having fun, there are ways of maximising reliability that won't cost anything other than time. Stripping the kart down after each race, cleaning every piece and putting it together again ensures everything is back the way it should be. Of course, you may find one or

two parts need replacing in the process and that will obviously require more cash, but the benefits of turning up at the track with a kart that you know is in the best shape it can be despite your team's limited budget is worth the effort. Let's not forget either, that it gives you an advantage over any team that may not have gone to the same dedicated lengths.

Good prep and regular maintenance is essential. Pulling out of a race because of a loose spark plug or steering column shouldn't occur. Before getting to the track, go through a maintenance checklist after rebuilding the kart and check everything that should be tight is so. Then check this again at the circuit, particularly before any race heat.

It is a good idea to stick to standard pieces of equipment. In an emergency in which you need to borrow, say, a wheel from another team, having an unusual sized rim will make this considerably less likely and could mean you having to sit out the rest of the day.

ABOVE Engines account for some of the highest karting costs. *(Author)*

OPPOSITE Get into the habit of stripping, cleaning and rebuilding your kart after every meeting. *(Enver Meyer)*

Of course, don't forget it's not just the kart that needs maintenance. Drivers should look after their equipment, too. Overalls need washing, gloves are likely to need replacing on a reasonably regular basis while helmets and visors should be carefully cleaned using the appropriate products.

Tools

As with any leisure activity in which you own equipment, running your kart means you'll inevitably accumulate a considerable amount of tools over time, but to start things off, you don't need as much as you may think. At the track you should initially get away with just the following:

- Screwdriver set
- Spanner set – specifically, 10mm, 13mm and 17mm
- Allen key set
- Good quality pressure gauge
- Spark plug spanner
- Long reach ratchet and socket set
- Cordless drill
- Pliers (standard and circlip)
- Funnel
- Fuel can
- Glass measuring jug (for two-stroke fuel/oil mix)
- Hammers (small and large)
- Rubber mallet
- Tape measure
- Gaffer tape
- Large supply of cable ties
- Larger selection of nuts, lock nuts, washers and bolts
- Chain lube
- WD40
- Selection of different sized sprockets and chains (if competing at various circuits)
- Two-stroke oil (mix with petrol if using two-stroke kart)
- Spare spark plug
- Spare chain
- Cleaning fluids and rags
- Foot pump
- Set of wet tyres (ideally mounted on rims)

In addition, the following tools are not vital but they will certainly make aspects of your karting life far easier:

- Laser tracking kit
- Wrench gun
- Compressor
- Generator
- Tyre temperature gauge
- Tyre softness tool
- Tyre press

Obviously, even having everything in the above two lists won't cover every eventuality but you'll be well on your way. The next step is to concentrate on tools that may be specifically required by the type of kart you own, but on a final general note, you should consider duplicating certain tools that you're likely to need simultaneously, such as the spanner set and even the wrench gun. The time these will save you in just one endurance pit stop is worth their cost alone.

LEFT Petrol and skin really don't get on, even with a kart suit layer between them, so invest in a funnel. *(Enver Meyer)*

BELOW Remember to choose your pit bay strategically. *(Darren Bourne)*

10

Sponsorship

Introduction

In reality, finding money to race may turn out to be the hardest challenge you'll face in karting. Particularly when you consider the level at which you'll start your karting career, which is likely to comprise local races and possibly county-level championships. If it's any consolation, even the guys at the top of the national series aren't exactly snowed under by offers of sponsorship. That shouldn't come as a surprise given that sponsors are hard to find at any level of motorsport.

One important point to remember when pitching for sponsorship is that at this level your focus should be on potential exposure rather than the promise of race results. Not that anyone likes to sponsor a team without success, obviously, but it is important to accept that from the perspective of an outsider – and specifically one who may have little or no understanding of the intricacies of karting – winning local races is never going to be as prestigious as getting on the podium steps after finishing the Monaco GP, for instance. The interest a sponsor will show a starter karting team, then, will be based almost entirely on what they'll get in return for their money, and what they'll be after is advertising, which is a blunter way of saying 'exposure'. It's actually the very basics of all sponsorship, let's not forget, but often the focus gets diluted with egos and emotions getting in the way when the big budgets start rolling in.

But that's something to worry about when you eventually get to F1. For now, if you're racing locally,

you'll need to think locally. There's little point approaching a nationwide company asking for support if you only race within the boundaries of your own county – any potential exposure will be of little benefit to them, after all. You're therefore far better concentrating on regional businesses and putting a convincing case together for why they should hand over their cash.

It's worth noting that, often, the sponsorship you'll see on karts is as a result of a business belonging to an acquaintance of the driver. So before targeting complete strangers, consider the people you know first. There may be an opportunity for sponsorship that will be comparatively effortless to arrange.

Preparation

Unless you have very rich friends, though, you're going to have to try to get a few more people on board, so be prepared. Don't contact a company without knowing what you're willing to offer and at what cost. Be realistic about the sums involved by basing these on the actual costs and keep in mind the fact that you may need to adapt your figures according to the company that you are dealing with.

For that you will need to learn as much about the company you're approaching and work out in advance the angle you're going to take – the 'sales pitch', if you like – in order to potentially get their interest.

Ideally, put together a sponsorship prospectus using a desktop publishing program (or similar

OPPOSITE It's important to realise how difficult securing sponsorship is – even drivers running at the front of some of the higher-profile series find it hard to get financial support. *(Enver Meyer)*

LEFT If you're racing locally, target local companies with any sponsorship proposals. *(Greg Richardson)*

presentation based software such as PowerPoint, for example) and get it printed on good quality paper, detailing your achievements to date, race plan for the next season and a variety of sponsorship options. A lot in business is about image and presenting yourself in a professional manner, while by no means a guarantee of success, can go a long way to securing a deal.

Promotion

Do your own PR. Before getting in touch with companies about potential sponsorship you'll want to have certain elements in place, not least so that you can refer to these as proof of potential exposure for your sponsor.

Assuming you're already gaining some success on the track, set up your own website and update it regularly with press releases detailing your progress. If you have talent, chances are you'll improve quickly and some of the main karting sites may eventually pick up on one your stories and run it, particularly if you're competing in a popular series or get involved with a charity race event. You will obviously need to keep them abreast of your developments for that to happen so email them regularly to point them towards new updates.

But in this age of social media it would seem silly not to use such a powerful tool to your advantage, too. So if a blog is too time consuming (no one said sponsorship would be easy, mind), consider at

least regular updates on facebook, Twitter or whichever social network solution keeps you online, share pictures with your contacts, upload videos onto YouTube and generally use the vast communication potential of the internet to your advantage. It all counts as exposure and you never know which of your friends just happens to have a wealthy, motorsport-loving uncle.

A local business with little interest in online activity, however, is more likely to be impressed with coverage gained in the local press. This requires a more proactive approach, as the majority of local newspapers have little or no interest in karting and convincing them otherwise is a hugely difficult task – although, granted, recent UK success at F1 level may carry a little influence. Ultimately, this is really an option that is only likely to work in a smaller town, where the sense of community tends to be stronger.

If that is your situation, inviting one of the journalists for a meeting over lunch to present your case as to why karting (specifically, your karting team) should become part of their publication's coverage is a good tactic. They are unlikely to rush back to the office to write up a profile of your team, granted, but at least you will have a contact to send your press releases to directly, rather than a generic newsdesk address. When doing so, always include a good picture to illustrate the potential article – a great image can do much to convince an editor to go with a story. Besides having a deadline, with only a very limited time to get the publication finished and sent off to the printers, the story without the picture will tend to be the one that gets dropped.

You may find that most of your initial press releases go unnoticed but assuming your progress on the track continues, then the possibility of eventually being featured in the local paper is strong. This is certainly the case if you manage to win your first championship (or are in a dramatic fight to the finish duel against another competitor) It is your responsibility to transmit this in your writing and without wishing to sound cynical, interest may also come if you get involved with a charity karting event. Local papers find charity-related stories of their community impossible to resist and are more likely to feature such an article, particularly if you manage to raise a considerable sum of money. They get their story, you get the coverage and a great day of racing, and the charity gets the money. Everyone is happy.

Getting the first article printed is the hardest part. From then on, the likelihood of further stories increases significantly – exposure usually creates further exposure, and local newspapers tend to like to follow up on subjects from past articles, particularly when they feature sporting achievements. But unless you tell people about yourself, no-one else is going to do it for you. There is the option of hiring a dedicated PR agency of course, but that should not be a consideration other than for those prepared to get very serious about their karting, and already at a certain level of competition.

Timing

The timing has to be right. Knocking on the door of businesses just as you've set up a karting team isn't ideal. You'll want to have gained results that demonstrate you're not always out of a race on the first lap. Equally, bear in mind companies work out their budgets at least a year in advance (and usually longer) so you also have to take that into account.

Also, if you manage to secure a meeting with someone from the company you will want to maximise the offers of exposure you can present. This means strategies such as the website and local press coverage discussed above, and that will require setting up well in advance of any sponsorship quest being undertaken.

Know your target

Not all small businesses will be familiar with sponsorship opportunities and will not therefore have set up a provision for such a venture (although there is a potential benefit for them with regards to their contribution possibly being tax deductible). So you will probably find after contacting these organisations that all you have is a long list of people who have promised to get back to you, the majority of which you'll never hear from again.

One way of minimising the 'we'll get back to you' scenario is to be specific about who you're targeting. Whenever possible, try to get in touch or

BELOW Organise 'corporate days' to enable current or potential sponsors to get a taste of the action. *(Enver Meyer)*

secure a meeting with the head of the business – you will want to deal with the decision maker rather than one of their subordinates and this is not unrealistic when dealing with small companies. Larger corporations will have a marketing director with control over a budget, but for smaller enterprises most expenditure will go through the boss.

The meeting

Having secured a meeting (don't underestimate the fact this will take great perseverance, but it is not impossible), be enthusiastic, be courteous and obviously try to appeal to their commercial side – your chances are likely to improve considerably if you understand the company's business and present yourself and your 'business offer' accordingly.

In all likelihood, they will have little or no desire to give you money. But if you sense things are going reasonably, as an incentive it may be an idea to invite them down to a race, or perhaps better still, to a practice day when you can

ABOVE Team shirts are affordable and provide a professional touch. *(Enver Meyer)*

RIGHT Always maximise the areas on a kart available for sponsor exposure. *(Greg Richardson)*

arrange some track time for them. Often, getting a potential sponsor to experience karting first-hand can do wonders for their sudden-found enthusiasm for the sport, and, hopefully, their impulsive desire to support a local kart team.

Of course, getting them to the track is the dream scenario. In truth, you're more likely to have to work hard to convince them within the restrictive environment of a meetings room. So practice your pitch before you go in. Concentrate on selling the positive – the exposure opportunities for their business or indeed any other angle that could potentially benefit their operation. For instance, a local tyre company is more than likely to be able to obtain kart tyres and supply these for you free, or at the very least at trade cost, in return for a couple of their logos on your kart. It's hardly going to cover your yearly running costs but it all adds up and is obviously infinitely better than having to pay for everything yourself.

Exposure

The type of exposure you offer will suit certain businesses better than others, but in addition to the typical areas involving race suit patches, lid visor strip and kart vinyl stickers, consider the following options:

- A sponsor's logo displayed on the team vehicle effectively transforms your transport into a moving advert. Given the miles the average karting team covers each year going to and from race meetings, the exposure opportunity is considerable.
- Prominent team website presence with banner and link to sponsor's own internet site.
- Product evangelising (where applicable).
- Corporate days for the sponsor (and, if applicable, its clients) to try out the kart on one of the championship circuits.
- The incorporation of the sponsor into the official team name, thereby guaranteeing exposure in the championship and karting websites, as well as potential television and press coverage.

Got the money

If you get as far as this, the work doesn't stop. In fact, it's probably just begun. Unless you're dealing with a philanthropist organisation, having put some money in your, sponsor will no doubt

like to see the benefits. This is when you have to ensure you guarantee them the maximum amount of exposure.

You will need to keep your sponsor up to date with your karting achievements. This is easily done through regular press releases and you should also draw their attention to their presence on your website and, of course, any media coverage you may be earning. As mentioned earlier, the latter obviously requires a significant energy investment.

You will need to keep your sponsor up to date with your karting achievements. This is easily done through regular communication – be it press releases, website or social media updates, or even pointing them to any media coverage you may be earning.

Keeping the sponsor involved by inviting them to races, for instance, is another good way to ensure good communication is maintained and the sponsor doesn't feel as though you've simply taken the money and run.

Ultimately, when it comes to sponsorship it is important to be aware that keeping a sponsor is almost as difficult as finding one in the first place. However, the ability to get to a race for little personal outlay, or finding the additional financial support needed to compete in the series of your choice more than compensates the considerable effort necessary to secure a sponsorship deal.

ABOVE Securing sponsorship is usually extremely hard work – even for those with supreme talent who get signed to a premier team's racing programme.
(Enver Meyer)

11

Racing parents

(Photo: Chris Walker)

Introduction

While people come to karting in all shapes and ages, there has been a noticeable increase in the number of youngsters turning up at tracks up and down the country. Part of this will no doubt be a result of karting's growing reputation. But you can't help wondering how much is the result of parents hoping they have the next Hamilton or Vettel on their hands.

The introduction of the Bambino class (see Chapter 1) has meant karting has never been so accessible by so many, so young. This chapter, then, is aimed primarily at the understandably enthusiastic racing mums and dads as a way to help them better understand the extent and impact of their involvement in their children's karting, whether as a fun, character-building activity or the start of a meticulously planned racing career.

No 'I' in 'team'

Depending on how serious you're expecting your child's karting to become, it's worth realising as early as possible what your role as a karting parent may involve. At its most extreme, you will be the agent/manager, the bank manager, the principle (or only) financier, cook, taxi driver, supporter, coach, practice partner, nurse, mechanic, tactician, counsellor, fan, laundry service and more.

You don't have to be Ross Brawn to work out that kind of multitasking is beyond the ability of mere mortals – at least if every aspect is going to be fulfilled as it should be. For that to happen (on the assumption that your child's karting is to be more than a hobby) you're going to need support from a dedicated team of professionals. That will of course mean relinquishing control of some crucial areas, which in practice can be a difficult thing to achieve for a parent that's been heavily involved from the moment their little one first slid into a Bambino seat. But for the team dynamic to work, parents will have to accept that they must let managers manage and coaches coach. Getting to know the other parents often helps because they are likely to be going through the same scenario and together you end up forming a support network to fall back on.

Supporting role

Just like the child will have to be realistic about the huge level of dedication that a motorsport career demands – and appreciate the sacrifices and efforts being made by those around them – parents must also be honest about the level of their involvement. This is crucial because it carries a direct impact on the child. An under-involved mum or dad that shows general disinterest in their child's activity will create a karter who lacks confidence, feels neglected and under-performs. Conversely, an over-involved parent will be overly focused on winning, critical and excitable, a character that's then reflected in an anxious, aggressive child who is a bad loser.

The perfect scenario involves a confident and balanced child that is reassured by a moderately involved parent that is supportive,

ABOVE Any young karter in a team should appreciate that their success will be due to the efforts of many. (Chris Walker)

LEFT A parent's level of involvement will have a direct effect on their child's karting, even at the Bambino stage. Over-involvement is undesirable, but alas all too common. (Chris Walker)

OPPOSITE If the racing bug really bites, expect the level of commitment to make considerable demands on all aspects of family life. (Chris Walker)

RIGHT With the right parental support, karting can be a wonderful source of self-confidence for youngsters, as well as a hugely enjoyable activity. *(Chris Walker)*

focused on the child and a good listener.

Support is the most important aspect a parent can bring to this environment. Whether winning or losing, being able to discuss the situation while giving plenty of encouragement by recognising the effort in addition to the achievement – as well as offering constructive criticism – is the key to becoming a positive role model. It's as critical a position within the team as it is demanding. If the karting bug takes hold, it will take considerable effort to balance out motorsport alongside everyday life, school, and normal family time.

School's in

Possibly the biggest disruption a serious karting involvement will cause a youngster is to their academic life. Aside from potentially spending every weekend racing at national level – which inevitably impacts on homework and general studies – continued success will eventually require frequent trips abroad to international competitions, meaning days off school. It is imperative to get the school onside as early as possible so prior to the start of the school year find out the training and race demands for your child's kart class, then set up a meeting with the headteacher to discuss your plans for the months ahead. Get them to realise how important this is for you and your child while presenting them with a solution that works for all (such as catch up missed lessons or even sitting exams that have a tendency to turn up just as a major championship is to be contested). Keep the school in the loop and nurture that relationship so that they can be supportive. With proper communication and planning most schools will prove themselves surprisingly flexible in their arrangements and a solid education is key because it becomes the back-up life plan if/when the motorsport career finishes. Because talent alone is no guarantee of rubbing nosecones against the Buttons, Alonsos and Kubicas of this world – so whether you're a clubman rookie or a KF1 supremo, remember to enjoy the karting.

BELOW Purchasing new karting kit for the very young – particularly Bambino equipment – isn't necessarily the wisest of investments, particularly when barely-used kit is easily found. *(Author)*

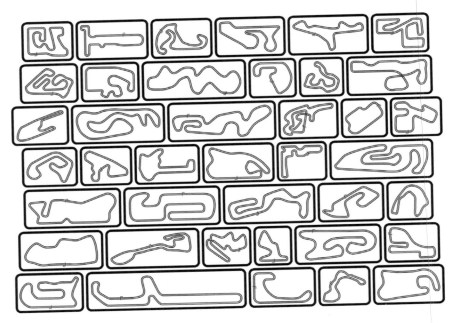

Appendix 1

The circuits

The good news for anyone wishing to go karting is that there are dedicated circuits all over the world, so you should find one not too far away from where you live. Not all circuits run all classes, or offer a licence test and only a selection are officially approved. Nevertheless, that doesn't mean you should immediately dismiss tracks that don't meet these criteria as there is usually plenty of great racing to be had. Standard do vary, of course, so some trial and error may be required. Here you'll find a selection of UK and popular international outdoor tracks covering a broad spectrum of classes.

UK

Ancaster Kart Racing (1200m)
Wood Lodge, Ancaster, Grantham, Lincolnshire
NG32 3PY
Telephone: 01400 230306
Email: info@ancasterkarting.co.uk
Website: www.ancasterkarting.co.uk

Anglia Karting Centre (1030m)
The Airfield, North Pickenham, Swaffham, Norfolk
PE37 8LL
Telephone: 01760 441777
Email: angliakarting@aol.com
Website: www.anglia-karting.co.uk

Bayford Meadows (1100m)
Symmonds Drive, Eurolink Industrial Estate, Sittingbourne,
Kent ME10 3RY
Telephone: 01795 410707
Email: info@bayfordkarting.co.uk
Website: www.bayfordkarting.co.uk

Brentwood Park Karting (825m)
The Racetrack, Brentwood Leisure Park, Warley Gap,
Brentwood, Essex CM13 3DP
Telephone: 01277 260001
Email: enquiries@brentwood-karting.com
Website: www.brentwood-karting.com

Buckmore Park Karting (1200m)
Maidstone Road, Chatham, Kent ME5 9QG
Telephone: 01634 201562
Email: sales@buckmore.co.uk
Website: www.buckmore.co.uk

Camberley Kart Club (660m)
Blackbushe Airport, Camberley, Surrey GU17 9LG
Telephone: 01276 512691
Website: www.camberleykartclub.com

Clay Pigeon Kart Club (815m)
Wardon Hill, Dorchester, Dorset DT2 9PW
Telephone: 01458 841100
Email: comp_sec@claypigeonkartclub.com
Website: www.claypigeonkartclub.com

Cumbria Kart Racing Club (1030m)
50 Newton Road, Dalton in Furness, Cumbria LA15 8NF
Telephone: 01229 463748
Email: mail@cumbriakrc.co.uk
Website: www.cumbriakrc.co.uk

Daytona Milton Keynes (1360m)
H4 Dansteed Way, Rooksley, Milton Keynes,
Buckinghamshire MK13 8NP
Telephone: 0845 644 5503
Email: mk@daytona.co.uk
Website: www.daytona.co.uk

Daytona Sandown Park (900m)
More Lane, Esher, Surrey KT10 8AN
Telephone: 0845 644 5502
Email: sandown@daytona.co.uk
Website: www.daytona.co.uk

Dunkeswell Kart Racing Club (Mansell Raceway)
Dunkeswell Aerodrome, Honiton, Devon, EX14 4LT
Telephone: 0844 544 0054
Website: www.dunkeswellkartclub.co.uk

Ellough Park Raceway (1050m)
Benacre Road, Ellough, Nr Beccles, Suffolk,
NR34 7XD
Telephone: 01502 717718
Website: www.elloughparkraceway.co.uk

Forest Edge Kart Club (1100m)
Barton Stacey, Hampshire SO21 3BF
Telephone: 01258 451097
Email: compsec@fekc.co.uk
Website: www.fekc.co.uk

Glan y Gors Park (1100m)
Glan-y-Gors Park, Cerrigydrudion, Corwen, Conwy
LL21 0RU
Telephone: 01490 420770
Email: edavies@gygkarting.co.uk
Website: www.gygkarting.co.uk

Golspie Kart Circuit (1100m)
North of Scotland Kart Club, Golspie, Little Ferry,
Golspie, Sutherland
Telephone: 01408 633459

Grand Prix Karting – Birmingham Wheels (1130m)
Adderley Road South, Birmingham, West Midlands B8 1AD
Telephone: 0121 3277700
Email: club@grandprixkarting.co.uk
Website: www.grandprixkarting.co.uk

Grampian Kart Club (860m)
Boyndie Drome, Banff, Grampian AB45 2LS
Telephone: 01467 624751
Email: secretary@grampiankartclub.com
Website: www.grampiankartclub.com

Hooton Park Circuit
Hooton Airfield, West Road, Ellesmere Port CH65 1BR
Telephone: 0151 355 7513
Website: www.hootonparkcircuit.co.uk

Hunts Kart Racing Club (1050m)
The Old Airfield, Stow Longa, Kimbolton,
Cambridgeshire PE28 0HU
Telephone: 01480 212210
Email: info@hkrc.co.uk
Website: www.hkrc.co.uk

Karting North East (1200m)
Warden Law Motorsport Centre, Sunderland,
Tyne & Wear SR3 2PR
Telephone: 0191 5214050
Email: info@kartingnortheast.com
Website: www.kartingnortheast.com

Kinsham Raceway (900m)
Lower Kinsham, Nr Presteigne, Herefordshire LD8 2HN
Telephone: 01544 267006
Website: www.kinshamraceway.co.uk

Lakeside Karting (900m)
Arterial Road (A1306), Thurrock, Essex
RM19 1EA
Telephone: 01708 863070
Email: sales@lakeside-karting.com
Website: www.lakeside-karting.com

Lincolnshire Kart Racing Club (950m)
Nr Stragglethorpe, Fulbeck, Lincolnshire LN5 0QZ
Telephone: 01142 302381
Email: secretary@lkrc.uk.com
Website: www.lkrc.uk.com

Llandow Kart Club (1050m)
Nr Llandwit Major, Glamorgan, CF71 7PB
Telephone: 01446 795568
Website: www.llandowkarting.co.uk

Lydd International Raceway (1240m)
Dengemarsh Road, Lydd, Romney Marsh, Kent
TN29 9JH
Telephone: 01797 321895

P.F. International Kart Circuit (1040m)
Brandon, Grantham, Lincolnshire NG32 2AY
Telephone: 01636 626424
Email: adrian@jmkartsport.co.uk
Website: www.jmkartsport.co.uk

Pro-Am Outdoor Karting (700m)
Tockwith Airfield, York, North Yorkshire
YO26 7QF
Telephone: 01423 359399
Email: tockwithkartschool@gmail.com
Website: www.proam-karting.co.uk

Raceland (930m)
Upper Diamond, Gladsmuir, East Lothian
EH33 1EJ
Telephone: 01875 853550
Email: mail@raceland.co.uk
web: www.raceland.co.uk

Red Lodge Karting (1200m)
Bury St Edmunds, Suffolk, IP28 8LE
Telephone: 01638 552316
Email: racing@redlodgekarting.com
Website: www.redlodgekarting.com

Rissington Kart Club (970m)
Nr Great Rissington, Cheltenham,
Gloucestershire GL54 2LR
Telephone: 01684 299292
Email: compsec@rissykartclub.com
Website: www.rissykartclub.com

Rye House Kart Raceway (950m)
Rye Road, Hoddesdon, Hertfordshire
EN11 0EH
Telephone: 01992 460895
Email: info@rye-house.co.uk
Website: www.rye-house.co.uk

Shenington Kart Circuit (1211m)
Shenington Airfield, Nr Banbury, Oxfordshire
OX15 6NW
Telephone: 01926 812177
Email: graham@sheningtonkrc.co.uk
Website: www.sheningtonkrc.co.uk

St Eval Kart Circuit (1200m)
St. Eval, Wadebridge, Cornwall PL27 7UN
Telephone: 01637 860160
Website: www.stevalkartcircuit.com

Stretton (800m)
Leicester Airport, Gartree Road, Great Stretton,
Leicestershire LE2 2FG
Telephone: 0116 2592900
Email: info@strettoncircuit.co.uk
Website: www.strettoncircuit.co.uk

Surbiton Raceway (720m)
Surbiton Town Sports Club, Rivermill Estate,
Worcester Park, Surrey KT4 7QB
Telephone: 0208 3375550
Email: surbraceway@btconnect.com
Website: www.surbiton-raceway.co.uk

Sutton Circuit (600m)
Sutton Elms, Nr Broughton Astley, Leicestershire LE9 6QF
Telephone: 01455 287078
Email: karts@suttoncircuit.co.uk
Website: www.suttoncircuit.co.uk

Teeside Karting (1300m)
South Tees Motor Sports Park, South Bank Road,
Middlesborough, Cleveland TS6 6XH
Telephone: 01642 231117
Email: information@teessidekarting.co.uk
Website: www.teessidekarting.co.uk

Three Sisters Race Circuit (1600m)
Three Sisters Road, Ashton-in-Makerfield, Wigan
Lancashire WN4 8DD
Telephone: 01942 270230
Email: info@three-sisters.co.uk
Website: www.three-sisters.co.uk

Thruxton Kart Centre (1100m)
Thruxton Circuit, Andover, Hampshire SP11 8PW
Telephone: 01264 882231
Email: karting@thruxtonracing.co.uk
Website: www.thruxtonkarting.co.uk

Ulster Karting Club (1000m)
11 Dundrod Road (B101), Nutts Corner, Crumlin,
Co. Antrim
Telephone: 07412 530778
Website: www.ulsterkartingclub.co.uk

West of Scotland Kart Club (850m)
Merryton Road, Larkhall, Hamilton, Strathclyde ML9 2UL
Telephone: 07900 197149
Email: info@wskc.co.uk
Website: www.wskc.co.uk

Whilton Mill (1200m)
Whilton Locks, Nr Daventry, Northamptonshire
NN11 2NH
Telephone: 01327 843822
Email: info@whiltonmill.co.uk
Website: www.whiltonmill.co.uk/karting.php

Wildtracks (700m)
Chippenham Road, Kennett, Newmarket,
Suffolk CB8 7QJ
Telephone: 01638 750496
Email: brenda@wildtracksltd.co.uk
Website: www.wildtracksltd.co.uk/karting

MAINLAND EUROPE

Circuit du Grand Ouest (1220m)
61500 Aunay les Bois, Pays d'Essay, France
Telephone: +33 (0)2 33 27 65 87
Website: www.ouest-karting.fr

Circuit International Jean Brun (1500m)
ASK Varennes s/Allier
BP 25, 03150 Varennes sur Allier, France
Telephone: +33 (0)4 70 45 57 31
Website: www.karting-varennes.site-city.fr

Circuit Karting Alain Prost (1174m)
Automobile Club de l'Ouest, 72019 Le Mans,
Cedex 2, France
Website: www.circuitalainprost.com

Circuit Karting JPR (1500m)
Circuit de la Métropole, RD 954-Zone d'Activité du Bois
Dion 9, F – 59162 Ostricourt F, France
Telephone: +33 (0)3 27 89 90 50
Website: www.karting-lille-jpr.fr

Circuit Roger Gaillard (1170m)
Association Sportive de Karting d'Ancenis, L'Aubinière,
120, rue Morane Saulnier, 44150 Ancenis, France
Telephone: +33 (0)2 40 96 00 22
Website: www.ask-ancenis.fr

Circuito de Siena (1080m)
53019 Castelnuovo Berardenga (SI), Strada Vicinale
Valdibiena, 3, Italy
Telephone: +39 (0)577 352075
Website: www.pistainternazionalesiena.com

Circuito Internacional de Zuera
Carratera Nacional 330 - Km 521,
50800 Zuera Spain
Telephone: +34 (0)976 697 125
Website: www.circuitointernacionaldezuera.es

Circuito Internazionale d'Abruzzo (1600m)
Contrada Villa, Torre 2, 66026 Ortona (Chieti), Italy
Telephone: +39 (0)85 903 2328
Website: www.circuitointernazionaledabruzzo.com

Circuito Internazionale Napoli (1699m)
via Sarno-Palma, 84087 Sarno (SA), Italy
Telephone: +39 (0)81 968229
Website: www.circuitointernazionalenapoli.com

Genk Kart Circuit (1350m)
Genker Kart Vereniging V.Z.W.,Europalaan 555,
3600 Genk, Belgium
Tel.: +32 (0)89 65 81 82
Email: events@kartinggenk.be
Website: www.kartinggenk.be

Kartodromo Internacional de Braga (1286m)
Rua do Kartódromo, Palmeira, Apartado 221,
4711-911 Braga, Portugal
Telephone: +351 (0)253 607560
Website: www.kib.pt

Kartodromo Internacional do Algarve
Sitio do Escampadinho, Mexilhoeira Grande 8500,
130 Portimão, Portugal
Telephone: +351 (0)282 405 600
Website: www.autodromoalgarve.com.pt/

Kartodromo Val Vibrata
Via Botticelli 24 Fraz. Faraone,
64016 Sant'Egidio Alla Vibrata (TE), Italy
Telephone: +39 (0)861 841 355
Website: www.camminho.com

Kerpen Kart Club (1107m)
Kart Club Kerpen-Manheim, Steinheide Kartbahn
50170, Kerpen, Germany
Telephone: +49 (0)22 75/91 32 14
Website: www.kart-club-kerpen.de

La Conca (1250m)
SS16 Maglie-Otranto Km 989,
73036 Muro Leccese (Lecce), Italy
Telephone: +39 (0)836 35 45 30
Website: www.laconca.com

Monaco Kart Cup (1079m)
ACM, 23 Boulevard Albert 1er, Boîte postale 464,
98012 Monaco, Monte-Carlo
Telephone: +377 (0)9315 2600
Website: www.acm.mc

Pista Azzurra di Jesolo (1045m)
Via Roma Destra, 90 – 30016 Jesolo (Ve), Italy
Telephone: +39 (0)421 972471
Website: www.pistazzurra.it

Pista Salentina (1400m)
SP 91 – Torre San Giovanni, Ugento, Italy
Telephone: +39 (0)833 931311
Website: www.pistasalentina.it

Prokart Raceland Wackersdorf (1275m)
Industriestr. 8, 92442 Wackersdorf, Germany
Telephone: +49 (0)94 31/755 20
www.prokart-raceland.com

RACB Karting Club (1070m)
Spa-Francorchamps, Route du Circuit, 51 B-4970
Stavelot, Belgium
Telephone: +32 (0)87 27 58 54
Website: www.francorchamps-karting.be

Rudskogen Motorcenter AS (1210m)
1890 Rakkestad, Norway
Telephone: +47 (0)69 22 68 10
Website: www.rudskogen.no

Sologne Karting (1500m)
Circuit International – RN 20, 41300 Salbris, France
Telephone: +33 (0)2 54 97 28 40
Website: www.sologne-karting.com

South Garda (1010m)
Via Monti Slossaroli s.n.c., 25017 Lonato del Garda (BS), Italy
Telephone: +39 (0)30 9919997
Website: www.southgardakarting.it

Templiner Ring (1102m)
Carl-Friedrich-Benz-Strasse 2,
17268 Templin/Uckermark, Germany
Telephone: +49 (0)3987 40 9960
www.kart-templin.de

Thy Motorsport Centre (1230m)
Højvang 29, 7700, Thisted, Denmark
Telephone: +45 (0)97 92 61 94
Website: www.tmsk.dk

Tibi Kart Motorsport (1197m)
Valchiavenna srl Pista Go Kart Via Boggia, 9 23020
Gordona (SO), Italy
Telephone: +39 (0)343.42540
Website: www.pistatibikart.it

Val d'Argenton Kart (1280m)
Circuit International du Val d'Argenton, La Folie
79150 Le Breuil Sous Argenton, France
Email: www.circuitvaldargenton.fr

WORLD

Adams Motorsports Park (1200m)
5298 Bell Ave, Riverside, CA 92509-2216, USA
Telephone: +1 951 686 3826
Website: www.adamsmotorsportspark.com

Albany City Kart (591m)
Albany Highway, Albany, Australia
Website: www.albanycitykartclub.com.au

Andersen RacePark (1600m)
Andersen Raceway Park, 10101 U.S. Highway 41 North,
Palmetto, FL 34221, USA
Telephone: +1 941 723 390
Website: www.andersenracepark.com

Bahrain International Kart Circuit (1414M)
Gate 255, Gulf of Bahrain Avenue, Umm Jidar

1062, Sakhir, Bahrain
Telephone: +973 17 450 000
Website: www.bahraingp.com

Ballarat Raceway (667m)
Racecourse Road, Haddon, Victoria, Australia
Website: www.ballaratkartclub.com

BeaveRun MotorSports Complex (1300m)
201 Penndale Road, Wampum, PA 16157, USA
Telephone: +1 724 535 1000
Website: www.beaverun.com

Blue Max Karting (2400m)
24998 Pole Line Road, Davis, California, USA
Website: www.bluemaxkartclub.com

Bolivar (755m)
Summer Road, Bolivar, Australia
Website: www.southernskc.asn.au

CalSpeed Karting Center (1210m)
9300 Cherry Avenue, Fontana, CA 92335, USA
Telephone: +1 951 506 9363
Website: www.calspeedkarting.com

Circleville Raceway Park (1120m)
19413 US Highway 23 North, 3113, USA
Telephone: +1 740 477 1626
Website: www.circlevilleraceway.com

G&J Kartway (800m)
1619 Barnets Mill Road, Camden, OH 45311, USA
Telephone: +1 937 452 1218
Website: www.gandjkartway.com

Geelong Karting Club (754m)
Beckley Park, Geelong Road, Corio, Victoria, Australia
Website: www.geelongkartingclub.com.au

Grand Junction Motor Speedway (1400m)
3030 N. I-70, Frontage Road, Grand Junction, CO
81504, USA
Telephone: +1 970 256 0107
Website: www.gjmotorspeedway.com

Gulf Coast Karters (1210m)
PO Box 19827, Houston, TX 77224, USA
Telephone: +1 281 978 3710
Website: www.racekarts.com

Gympie Gold (890m)
CCKC, 10 Runge Rd, Glanmire, QLD 4570, Australia
Website: www.cckc.org.au

Highclere (770m)
1498 Ridgeley Highway, Highclere, Tasmania, Australia
Website: www.nwkc.org.au

Ipswich Kart (1080m)
Champions Way, Willowbank, Queensland, Australia
Website: www.ipswichkartclub.com.au

Iron Rock Raceway (1170m)
10320 Hotel Drive, ABIA Building 7390, Austin,
TX 78719, USA
Telephone: +1 512 530 7223
Website: www.ironrockraceway.com

JET Karting (1120m)
3674 East 2603, Road, Sheridan, IL 60551, USA
Telephone: +1 815 496 9196
Website: www.jetkarting.com

Launceston Kart Club
Archerville Kartway, Pipers River Road,
Nr Launceston, Australia
Website: www.lkc.com.au

Lincoln County Raceway (1053m)
Newell Highway, Brocklehurst, Australia
Website: www.dubbokartclub.com

McMinnville Kart Track (960m)
2600 NE, McMinnville, OR 97128, USA
Website: www.portlandkarting.com

Michiana Raceway Park (1500m)
61870 Crumstown Highway, North Liberty,
IN 46554, USA
Telephone: +1 574 288 4922
Website: www.michianaracewaypark.com

Miller Motorsports Park (1430m)
2901 N. Sheep Lane, Tooele, Utah 84074, USA
Telephone: +1 435 277 7223
Website: www.millermotorsportspark.com

Monarto Kart Circuit (1050m)
Old Princes Highway, Monarto, South Australia
Website: www.gokartclubofsa.com

Monticello Karting (1700m)
1765 Big Joe Road, Monticello, Florida 32344, USA
Telephone: +1 850 510 4188
Website: www.monticellokarting.com

New Castle Motorsports Park (1600m)
5816 South County 125 West, New Castle, IN 47362,
USA
Telephone: +1 765 987 8090
Website: www.newcastleraceway.com

New Jersey Motorsports Park (1770m)
47 Warbird Drive, Millville, NJ 08332, USA
Telephone: +1 856 327 8000
Website: www.njmotorsportspark.com

Newcastle Kart Track (1058m)
5 Cameron Park Drive, Cameron Park, NSW 2285,
Australia
Website: www.nkrc.com.au

North Texas Karters (800m)
2119 Langston Court, Dallas, TX 75235, USA
Telephone: +1 940 482 3777
Website: www.ntkarters.com

Oakleigh Kart Circuit (960m)
Deals Road Reserve, Deals Road, Clayton, Australia
Website: www.ogkrc.com.au

Ocala Gran Prix (965m)
4121 NW 44th Ave, Ocala, FL 34482, USA
Telephone: +1 352 690 7223
Website: www.ocalagranprix.com

Phoenix Kart Racing (1210m)
23280 N 43rd Ave, Glendale, AZ 85083, USA
Website: www.pkra.com

Stockton Motorplex (800m)
Stockton, CA 95206, USA
Website: www.stocktonmotorplex.com

Rockhampton Kart Club (861m)
Fitzroy Park Raceway, Bruce Highway, Nr Rockhampton,
Australia
Website: www.rfkkc.com.au

Sheathers Road Track (750m)
Maloney Drive, Albury Wodonga, Australia
Website: www.kartracing.com.au

Suzuka Kart Circuit (1264m)
7992 Ino-Cho, Suzuka-shi, Mie-Ken 510-0295, Japan
Telephone: +81 59 378 3620
Website: www.mobilityland.co.jp

Todd Road (1005m)
Port Melbourne, Victoria, Australia
Website: www.gkcv.com.au

Wimmera Kart Circuit (580m)
Dooen Raceway, 650 Henty Hwy, Dooen (Horsham),
Australia
Website: www.wimmerakartclub.com.au

Wundowie (752m)
Hurricane Kart Club, 99 Burma Rd, Wundowie, WA,
Australia
Website: www.hurricanegokartclub.net

Appendix 2

Useful addresses

This is by no means an exhaustive list of all the services related to buying, owning and racing a kart, but is intended to provide some guidance as well as an indication of the variety of the services available for those new to karting. While there is no implied guarantee with regards to the quality and ability of those listed, where applicable, they have been chosen carefully as a result of personal experience.

Organisations

As you would expect for a sport as established as karting, there are a number of organisations catering for all levels and areas of karting. The major examples are as follows.

Association of British Kart Clubs (ABkC)

Secretary: Graham Smith
Stoneycroft, Godsons Lane, Napton, Southam, Warwicks CV47 8LX
Telephone: 01926 812177
Email: secretary@abkc.org.uk
Website: www.abkc.org.uk

Formed in 1990, the ABkC represents many of the kart clubs in the UK. It is in close contact with the MSA and acts as an interface between its member clubs and the motorsport organisation. The regulations affecting its direct drive and gearbox championships are published on a yearly basis. Member clubs must adhere to these, enabling drivers to attend different clubs and still find the same classes. Competitors joining the ABkC become eligible to race at ABkC clubs and, subsequently, in the ABkC national championships.

Association of Racing Kart Schools (ARKS)

Telephone: 01926 812177
Email: secretary@arks.co.uk
Website: www.arks.co.uk

This is the UK trade association for the professional kart schools and is responsible for regulating these, together with administering the compulsory novice kart driver ARKS test needed to obtain an MSA licence. A list of the schools that are members of the association and therefore recognised by the Motor Sports Association can be found on the ARKS website.

British Kart Industry Association (BKIA)

PO Box 2122, Worthing, BN12 9DA
Telephone: 01903 241921
Email: info@bkia.co.uk
Website: www.bkia.co.uk

The BKIA represents the karting industry's manufacturers, retailers, circuits, associated businesses and organisations. It operates a strict code of conduct for its members.

British Superkart Association (BSA)

2 Lion Close, Norwich, Norfolk NR5 0UQ
Telephone: 01603 743563
Website: www.superkart.org.uk

The BSA runs alongside the ABcK and is responsible for the regulation of long circuit racing, including the MSA Long Circuit Kart Championship.

Commission Internationale de Karting (CIK)

2 Chemin de Blandonnet, CP 296, CH-1215, Genève 15, Switzerland
Telephone: +41 (0)22 306 1080
Website: www.cikfia.com

Specialised karting commission of the FIA overseeing karting safety in conjunction with the FIA institute for motorsport safety and with a research group exclusively dedicated to karting.

Fédération Internationale de l'Automobile (FIA)

2, Chemin de Blandonnet, 1215 Genève 15, Switzerland
Telephone: +41 (0)22 544 4400
Website: www.fia.com

The world governing body for motorsport, as well as representing the interests of motoring organisations and motor car users internationally.

Motor Sports Association (MSA)

Motor Sports House, Riverside Park, Colnbrook, Slough SL3 0HG
Telephone: 01753 765000
Email: kart@msauk.org
Website: www.msauk.org

The UK's sole governing body for motorsport, responsible for the administration and control of motorsport rules. It is recognised by the world governing body, the FIA.

National Karting Association (NKA)

Devonia, Long Road West, Dedham, Colchester, Essex CO7 6ES
Telephone: 01206 322726
Email: enquiry@nationalkarting.co.uk
Website: www.nationalkarting.co.uk

Set up to help, promote and protect operators of both indoor and outdoor karting circuits.

National Schools Karting Association (NatSKA)

Email: secretary@natska.co.uk
Website: www.natska.co.uk

A nationwide association that aims to increase the involvement of schools in karting. Race meetings are held throughout the country at major circuits and operate under strict MSA regulations.

World Karting Association (WKA)

6051 Victory lane, Concord, NC 28027, USA
Telephone: +1 704 455 1606
Website: www.worldkarting.com

North America's largest karting regulatory body that, alongside the IFK (see below) publishes the rules of competition for the US.

International Kart Federation (IFK)

1609 South Grove Avenue Suite 105, Ontario, California, 91761, USA
Telephone: +1 405 840 3158
Email: kartenews@ikfkarting.com
Website: www.ikfkarting.com

Exhibitions

KartMania

'The Wing', Silverstone Circuit,
Silverstone NN12 8TN (Venue can vary)
Email: info@kartmania.co.uk
Website: www.kartmania.co.uk

The UK's main annual karting exhibition, usually
held in December and enjoying good support
from all sectors of the karting industry. Typically,
it runs a series of useful workshops and
conferences for attendees in conjunction with
an increasing number of exhibitors, but it's
worth noting representatives from all corners of
the industry are also easily approachable on the
showfloor. In recent years a second-hand
section offers attendees the chance to pick up
some bargains.

Autosport International

The NEC Arena, Birmingham, B40 1NT
Website: www.autosportinternational.com

Yearly major motorsport exhibition traditionally held
in January with a sizeable section dedicated to
karting and attended by all leading manufacturers
and service providers. You will find these on hand
and willing to offer advice and information on the
latest equipment and competitions or even on how
to get started in this sport. Typically, karting
equipment retailers run a series of 'show special
offers' on much of their stock, so it can be a good
place to buy some new kit.

Internationale Kart-Ausstellung

Messe Offenbach, Kaiserstraße 108-112, D-63065
Offenbach, Germany
Website: www.kartmesse.de

Yearly event held in Germany since 1993, the
Internationale Kart-Ausstellung has grown to
claim the crown of the largest karting exhibition
in the world.

Related services

■ Driving tuition

Protrain Racing Products Ltd

6 Hillcrest Way, Buckingham Industrial Park,
Buckingham, Buckinghamshire, MK18 1HJ
Telephone: 01280 814774
Email: protrain@karttraining.co.uk
Website: www.protrainracing.co.uk

Long running ARKS kart driving school, offering a
selection of courses ranging from beginner to
international level. Chief instructor is Gary Chapman,
European and six-time National Kart Champion.
Additional services include full race hire options,
including storage, kart preparation, transportation,
consultancy and race engineer support.

EvenFlow Kart Driver Coaching

Telephone: 01536 799008
Email: terence@evenflow.co.uk
Website: www.evenflow.co.uk

A more personal style of driver coaching which,
since 2003, has focused as much on technical
aspects as a driver's psychological make-up.
Plenty of information is available on the site and,
ingeniously, even remote coaching is available
(by asking karters to send in on-board footage
of their driving).

iZone Karting Academy

2255 Silverstone Technology Park,
Silverstone Circuit, Silverstone NN12 8GX
Telephone: 01327 856872
Website: www.appm.co.uk/karting.html

The brainchild of triple World Touring Car
Champion Andy Priaulx, the iZone Academy
uses state-of-the-art training equiptment to
unlock a driver's inner potential.

■ Engine preparation

Ogden Motorsport

Becklands Close, Barr Lane, Boroughbridge, North
Yorkshire YO51 9LS
Telephone: 01423 324738
Email: steve@oms.gb.com
Website: www.ogdenracing.com

Kart engine preparation specialist, offering
tuning, rebuilds, new engines, and kart
preparation services.

Fitness training

Driver Performance

Prodrive, Banbury, Oxfordshire, OX16 3ER
Telephone: 01295 754008
Email: pwebster@prodrive.com
Website: www.driverperformance.co.uk

Physical conditioning and therapy specialist,
specifically tailored to the needs of motorsport
competitors. Offers an extensive programme,
including motorsport specific fitness assessment,
personal fitness training, nutrition planning,
chiropractic support, sport psychology
implementation and more.

Helmet design

JLF Designs

Unit 6, Shepherds Grove Industrial Estate, Stanton,
Bury St Edmunds, Suffolk IP31 2AR
Telephone: 01359 252225
Email: shirley@jlfdesigns.com
Website: www.jlfdesigns.com

Helmet painting specialist established in 1991,
responsible for designs featured on some of the
leading racing drivers across a variety of disciplines.

Insurance

MORIS

c/o Everitt Boles Ltd, Mint House, 1st Floor, 77
Mansell Street, London E1 8AF
Telephone: 020 7264 3324
Email: info@moris.co.uk
Website: www.kartinsurance.com

Specialist kart insurance company offering storage
and transit cover, chassis on-track damage, and
personal injury policies.

PR

100cc PR

Telephone: 01702 390348
Email: info@100ccpr.co..uk
Website: www.100ccpr.co.uk

Public relations company dedicated to building the
profile and exposure of kart drivers, as well as help
develop sponsorship opportunities.

Retailers

Demon Tweeks Direct

75 Ash Road South, Wrexham Industrial Estate,
Wrexham, Conwy LL13 9UG
Telephone: 08453 306241
Email: sales@demon-tweeks.co.uk
Website: www.demontweeks.co.uk

Grand Prix Racewear

Silverstone Retail & Mail Order, Unit 1, Silverstone
Technology Park, Silverstone Circuit,
Towcester, Northants NN12 8TN
Telephone: 01327 855585
Email: silverstone@grandprixracewear.com
Website: www.gprdirect.com

Karting Direct

Unit 11, King Street Industrial Estate, Langtoft,
Peterborough, PE6 9NF
Telephone: 01778 561061
Email: sales@kartingdirect.co.uk
Website: www.kartingdirect.co.uk

ProKart Engineering

6 Dunstable Walk, Fareham, Hants PO14 1SE
Telephone: 01329 289783
Email: info@prokart.co.uk
Website: www.prokart.co.uk

Tal-Ko Racing Ltd

54 Sunderland Road, Sandy, Bedfordshire, SG19 1QY
Telephone: 01767 682020
Email: info@tal-ko.com
Website: www.tal-ko.com

Tillett Racing Seats

3 Castleacres Industrial Park, Castle Road,
Sittingbourne, Kent ME10 3RZ
Telephone: 01795 420312
Email: info@tillett.co.uk
Website: www.tillett.co.uk

Zip Kart

Unit 1, Silverstone Tech Park, Silverstone Circuit,
Towcester NN12 8TN
Telephone: 01327 855310
Email: info@zipkart.com
Website: www.zipkart.com

Zoom Kartmart

Milward House, Eastfield Side, Sutton in Ashfield,
Nottinghamshire NG17 4JW
Telephone: 01623 512463
Email: sales@zoomkarts.com
Website: www.zoomkarts.com

Other useful contacts

www.karting.co.uk
The UK's most comprehensive website dedicated to karting.

www.karting1.co.uk
Passionate site covering all aspects of world karting, as well as providing a great deal of information and advice.

Karting Magazine
Moorfield House, 15 Moorfield Road, Orpington, Kent BR6 0XD
Telephone: 01689 897123
Email: support@kartingmagazine.com
Website: www.kartingmagazine.com

Club 100 & EasyKart UK
Bon Accord House, Castle Road, Eurolink Commercial Park, Sittingbourne, Kent ME10 3SJ
Telephone: 01795 422455
Email: racing@club100.co.uk
Website: www.club100.co.uk

Daytona Max
Telephone: 0845 644 5504
Email: max@daytona.co.uk
Website: www.daytonamax.co.uk

References and further reading

Motosport Fitness Manual
Jutley, Dr R. S. and Blow, Andy (Haynes, 2009)

Bob Bondurant on Race Kart Driving
Bondurant, Bob & Bentley, Ross (MBI, 2002)

Memo Gidley's Secrets of Speed Four-cycle Kart Racing
Grist, Jeff & Gidley, Memo (Secrets of Speed Publications, 2005)

Kart Chassis Set Up Technology
Smith, Steve (Steve Smith Autosports, 2002)

Inner Speed Secrets: Mental Strategies to Maximize Your Racing Performance
Bentley, Ross & Langford, Ronn (MBI, 2000)

Kart Driving Techniques
Hall II, Jim & Smith, Steve (Steve Smith Autosports, 1999)

Index